MW01248911

Visitor's Guide to Shakespeare Country

Including

Stratford-upon-Avon, Warwick, Kenilworth
and the Towns, Villages and Hamlets

By

Blair Howard

This guide focuses on outdoor and recreational activities. As all such activities contain elements of risk, the publisher, author, affiliated individuals and companies disclaim responsibility for any injury, harm, or illness that may occur to anyone through, or by use of, the information in this book. Every effort was made to insure the accuracy of information in this book, but the publisher and author do not assume, and hereby disclaim, liability for any loss or damage caused by errors, omissions, misleading information or potential travel problems caused by this guide, even if such errors or omissions result from negligence, accident or any other cause information or for any potential travel problems caused by this guide.

Important Note: The rates for accommodations – hotels, inns, pubs, bed & breakfast, etc. - fees, prices, and especially the entrance fees to the many attractions, quoted throughout this book were current at the time of writing. However, they are all subject to change without notice and they do, **almost weekly**, thus the prices quoted herein are given only as a rough guide as to what you might expect to pay. The author therefore disclaims any liability for such changes and urges you to check, either by phone or online for current rates before you travel.

Photo Credits:

Cover Photo: Ten Penny Cottage at Welford on Avon by Philip Halling. Back Cover: Anne Hathaway's Cottage by Tony Hisgett

All other photos, unless specifically identified are courtesy of Creative Commons.

Introduction

Shakespeare Country, the land of the Bard, encompasses most of the western reaches of the county of Warwickshire, along with the historic towns of Warwick, Kenilworth and a half-a-hundred towns, villages and hamlets, large and small, along with a section of the Eastern Cotswolds. It's a world unlike any other, historic and stunningly beautiful. This is the part of England where I grew up. I don't think there a town or village I haven't visited at one time or another, but from Warwick and Kenilworth, to Stratford and all points west, including the towns and villages of the Cotswolds, this is my world. I welcome you to it, and I hope you'll learn to love it as much as I do.

Beautiful even in winter - Anne Hathaway's Cottage - Photo Courtesy of Andy Kerridge .

The County of Warwickshire lies at the very heart of England. In fact the tiny village of Meriden, located between Birmingham and Coventry, claims to be the mathematical center of the nation. Be that as it may,

Warwickshire offers some of the most beautiful countryside to be found anywhere in Europe.

The Old Bridge over the River Avon at Warwick – Photo Courtesy of Roland Turner

The rolling hills and dales, and the tiny villages - some hardly more than a couple of cottages and a country store - carry on with life much as they did more than 400 years ago when the Bard of Avon strolled through the leafy glades of the forest of Arden. The great forest once covered most of Warwickshire; today almost all of it is gone, the victim of urban development. Only a few scattered fragments still remain, but they are more than enough to provide a window into what life must have been like in medieval England.

The River Avon, unspoiled and little changed from the way it was in Shakespeare's time, meanders southward from the ancient town of Warwick in the northeast, through the rolling countryside to Stratford-upon-Avon, then on through Bidford and Evesham until finally it links with the river Severn at Tewksbury.

In this idyllic backdrop, the inspiration for Shakespeare's "A Midsummer Night's Dream," you can lose yourself in an atmosphere so heavy with antiquity you can almost hear the faint voices of long ago echoing through the corridors of Warwick castle, or the tiny bedrooms of the Garrick Inn in Stratford-upon-Avon.

Warwick Castle – Photo Courtesy of Pam Brophy

The town of Stratford-upon-Avon dates back almost into the dark ages; the first settlement was Anglo-Saxon, but the original town charters were not granted until 1196. The name is a combination of the Old English words "strete and ford," Stratford, a place where the river could be forded, and the river was, of course, the Avon.

The Bridge that Replaced the Ford at Stratford – Photo Courtesy of Creative Commons

In Medieval times, the Bishops of Worcester ruled the area as lords of the manor. John de Coutances was the Bishop of Worcester in 1196 and in that year petitioned King Richard 1st (the Lionheart) for a charter to hold a weekly market in the town; thus merchants from around about could come to Stratford and trade their wares and goods; the charter was duly granted and so Stratford became a "market town."

And it was the Bishops of Worcester who first established the popular statute or "mop" fairs that are still held each year in Stratford on the twelfth day of October. If you live in any one of a dozen other towns in the area, you'll be very familiar with the local mop fair – they all have them - if not... well, maybe a little later in the book.

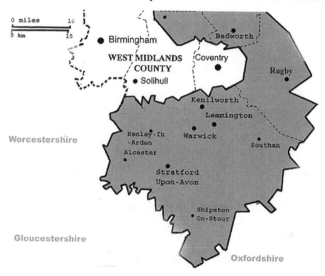

Map of Shakespeare Country – Courtesy of Creative Commons

Stratford-upon-Avon is obviously the focal point of Shakespeare Country, but there's so much more to it. For instance, Warwick and Kenilworth are two historic towns located just a few miles to the northeast of Stratford, both are steeped in history and both played important roles in the early development of England. Each has what once was a great castle; each castle was once home to some of the greatest of England's noblemen.

The town of Warwick is remarkable, not only for its great medieval castle, but also for its cathedral-like church. No visit to Shakespeare Country would be complete with a visit to both Warwick and Kenilworth.

Kenilworth Castle – Photo Courtesy of Creative Commons

If you're making a day trip visit from London, you'll just be able to visit only one or two of the highlights – Stratford, Warwick and perhaps Kenilworth. But if you have the time, and can visit for a week, you'll be able to visit all of the most popular places that claim to be a part of Shakespearian history. These include:

Ragley Hall – Photo Courtesy of Creative Commons

Ragley Hall, the home of the Marquess of Hartford, is one such place. Coughton Court is another, and has been the home of the Throckmorton family since 1409. Its claim to fame is the role it played in the Gunpowder Plot of 1605.

Then there are the Shakespearian villages immortalized in verse by the Bard himself: Piping Pebworth (Pebworth), Dancing Marston (Long Marston), Hungry Grafton (Temple Grafton), Dodging Exhall (Exhall), Papish Wixford (Wixford), Beggarly Broom (Broom), Drunken Bidford (Bidford-upon-Avon), and Haunted Hillsborough (Hillsborough).

Hinnington Spring Mill – Photo Courtesy of Creative Commons

You'll also have time enough to visit the idyllic English villages of Broadway and Stoneleigh, and the nearby Stoneleigh Abbey with its mediaeval gatehouse; then it's on to the small market towns of Alcester, Henley-in-Arden, Evesham, Chipping Campden and many more.

We will, however, begin with what Shakespeare Country is really all about, Stratford-upon-Avon and the man himself:

Table of Contents

If you're visiting Shakespeare Country from outside of the UK, this next section is for you. If you are vising from within the UK, you can skip this section.

Visas:

As of this writing, if you are a citizen of Australia, Canada, New Zealand, South Africa or the USA, you need a valid passport and will receive at your point of entry, 'leave to enter' the UK for up to six months. You will not be allowed to work in the UK unless you have a work permit. Citizen of the EU do not need a visa to enter the UK; they are also free to stay/live for as long as they like, and may work if they wish too.

UK Customs:

If you arrive in the UK from any country outside EU (European Union), you will have to comply with the UK Customs regulations. Countries belonging to the EU operate a "two-tier" customs system: one for duty free goods purchased outside the EU, and one for those purchased within the EU where the taxes and duties are paid at the point of purchase.

Visitors arriving from countries outside the EU are allowed to import:

• Tobacco: you may import 200 cigarettes or 50 cigars or 250g of tobacco, or any combination thereof.

• Alcohol: you may import 4 liters of non-carbonated wine *plus* 1 liter of spirits over 22% proof, OR 2 more liters of wine (sparkling wine if you like), and again you make up your alcohol allowance from any combination of alcohol products.

- Perfumes: there are no restrictions.
- Beer: the allowance is 16 liters of beer
- Electronics, Cameras and Souvenirs and other duty-free goods to the value of £300.

If you are arriving in the UK from an EU country, you can bring in a limited amount of duty-paid goods. Depending upon your country of origin, those goods may cost less than you would pay for them in the UK. Imported duty-paid items are deemed to be for "individual consumption," and that means there are limits to how much you can import into the UK:

- 800 cigarettes
- 200 cigars
- 1 kilo of tobacco
- 10 liters of spirits
- 20 liters of fortified wine (port, sherry etc.)
- 90 liters of wine, including no more than 60 liters of sparkling wine (Champagne etc.)
- 110 liters of beer

And, of course, there are a number of items banned by the UK Customs Service:

- Illegal drugs (cocaine, marijuana, heroin, morphine, etc.)
- Weapons (guns, flick knives, knuckledusters, swords, etc.)
- Pornographic material - other than that can legally be purchased in the UK
- Counterfeit goods and goods that infringe patents (handbags, watches, DVDs, CDs, etc.)
- Meat, milk and other animal products.

If you're planning a trip to The UK, staying in touch with the folks back home, planning your route, accessing the web, and so on and so forth, is an important consideration. That being so, the smart phone, and most of us have them these days, would seem to be the answer. Almost all smartphones will work in the UK, once you've activated your account to allow international access, that is. You'll be able to make calls, send texts, access the web, map your routes, and use your favorite apps. Unfortunately, all of which can be very expensive.

American smartphone users rarely think about the cost of roaming, data usage and such. Most of their packages come with virtually unlimited minutes and data. This is not the way it is when you travel abroad. When you place a call within the EU, your provider must connect to a local carrier to make the connection, and that comes with a cost. So... what to do?

Call your carrier and discuss your options and purchase an international plan for phone calls.

Without such a special plan, both AT&T and Verizon charge high per-minute rates: Verizon charges $1.29 per minute for calls you make or receive while in the UK. You can purchase Verizon's international calling plan for $4.99 per month which will reduce the cost to a little more manageable 99 cents per month; a similar plan offered by AT&T costs $5.99 per month – better, but still not cheap. Both plans allow you to check your emails.

Both Verizon and AT&T offer special data plans; you'll need one of those too. Verizon charges a base rate of $20.48 for one megabyte of data, but you can purchase data in 100 megabyte packages for $25 (overages cost $25 per 100MB); seems a silly not to do so.

9

If you don't plan on using data while traveling, go to "settings" in your device and turn Data Services off.

And speaking of that, you should always turn off your phone when you're not using it. If your phone rings while you're in the UK, you will be charged by the minute, even if you don't answer it.

Dialing the U.S.

Dial the Plus Sign (+) then 1 then enter ten digit U.S. number

Mapping Your Route

Using the GPS feature of your smart phone for mapping your routes comes out of your data package, so you'll need to be very careful; you also need to be remember that while you're are using the mapping software, your phone is on and can receive calls, for which you will be charged even if you don't answer them (1 minute minimum).

Texting: Texting today is more popular than making a call. Verizon does not have a special plan for texting; they charge $.50 to send and $.05 to receive a text message in the EU. No special plans or deals. AT&T's plan is a little different. Without their international texting plan, you will be charged $.50 to send a text, but that can drop as little as $.10 each if you purchase their $50 international texting plan - 500 text messages.

Pay as You Go Mobile Phones

Pay as you go is a terrific option for visitors to the EU. I used this option on my last visit to Paris. I simply purchased a SIM card for my phone: not a smartphone, just a regular Blackberry. There are no specific plans for the pay as you go option, you simply buy credit from phone centers at newsagents with "Top-Up" signs in their windows.

Check with your phone company and find out which UK SIM cards will work in your phone. UK SIM cards cost £5-£10. If your phone is not compatible, no problem: you can purchase a pay as you go phone in the UK for £50 to £100 each. The most popular mobile phone companies in the UK are: T-Mobile, Virgin Mobile, and Vodaphone. These are the premier providers, but there are others. The cost of mobile calls varies according to the provider; text messages within the UK cost about 10p.

About Money

The UK unit of currency is the pound sterling (£), often called a "quid" by the locals, thus something that costs £2 would be a couple of quid, in local terms.

At the time of writing, the Pound is worth $1.66 U.S. Yes, you will get £1 for each $1.66 you exchange, but don't let that fool you. On my many journeys home to the UK, I have found that what might cost $1 in the U.S. might well cost £1 in the UK. Thus the cost of many goods and goodies in the UK can be confusing. Also, do not fall into the trap, as many foreigners do, of thinking £1 = $1. You will soon run out of funds if you do.

Currency Exchange

It's never been easier to change your money into UK pounds, and the costs to exchange it have never been more wide ranging. You can change your money many different sources, at home and in The UK. These would include airports, banks, travel agencies and street kiosks, all of them are in business to make a profit. Always check the current rate of exchange before you make a deal. The best rates are usually available at local banks; the worst rates are at the airport (very tempting, but probably the most expensive option), the currency exchange kiosks in the city of London, and at the railway stations. I usually exchange some of my dollars at my local bank in the U.S. before leaving the States. This gives me a good rate of exchange, and some ready cash for bus, Tube and taxi fares, and snacks, when I arrive in The UK. Then I will make a bigger buy at one of the local banks, such a Lloyds or Barclays.

Traveler's Checks:

Traveler's checks are the best and safest way to carry your money. I take most of my cash in the form of traveler's checks, almost always purchased from American Express directly, mainly because of the worldwide support and availability of local Amex offices in London and other major cities.

Always buy your traveler's checks in UK pounds. If not, you'll be required to pay exchange fees when you change them in The UK.

Credit and Debit Cards

Credit cards, and most debit cards, are universally accepted in the UK. But you will need some cash as well, to pay for snacks, coffees, and local transportation. Use your credit cards to pay for large items, hotels, eating out, car rentals etc., and use your debit card to get the cash you need at an ATM machine (see below) That way, you'll always get the best rate of exchange, and you won't need to carry around large amounts of cash.

ATM Machines:

Personally, I have never had a problem finding an ATM machine in The UK, or elsewhere in the EU. If you have to ask for directions to the nearest ATM, you will need to remember to ask for a 'cash machine' or a 'cash point.' I tend to rely heavily on my debit card, not only is it quick and easy, you'll get the best rate of exchange when the charges get back to own bank.

How to Get There

I am assuming that you'll be arriving in England via one of London's airports, and that you'll be traveling to Shakespeare country from there, either for the day, or for a longer stay. There are several travel options you might like to consider. Me? I always go by road, but the train is cheaper, often easier, and certainly more scenic.

By Road

Stratford-upon-Avon is roughly 100 miles northwest of London via the M4, M25. M40 and A46 roads. It's a drive of about 2 hours 15 minutes. Take the M40 north to junction 15 - the A429/A46 (Stratford Road) - and dive on into Stratford; it's motorway driving almost all of the way so it's an easy run. Keep in mind that gasoline, called petrol in the UK, is very expensive (about $5 per gallon) and sold by the liter (a little more than a quart).

By Train

One of the best, and the cheapest, ways to get to Stratford is by train. Trains leave from London Marylebone Station about every two hours – up to five times per day in each direction - and up to seven times per day one way from London to Stratford. The trip takes 2 hours 15 minutes, with round trip advance fares starting about £10 (that is terrific value for money). Stratford Parkway railway station is located just to the north of the town within easy reach of the hotels via taxi.

Visit by Guided Tour

Premier Tours out of London offer several guided tours to Shakespeare Country. Go to premiertours.co.uk.

Stratford-upon-Avon

Stratford-upon-Avon, known locally as Stratford, is a small market town and popular tourist destination in southwest Warwickshire; it's even a popular tourist destination for folks who live no more than a dozen miles away.

Stratford owes its fame to just one man, the playwright and poet William Shakespeare. By an accident of this man's birth, Stratford enjoys an income from tourism that's probably second only to London. Each year, almost 5 million visitors from all over the world visit Stratford-upon-Avon. The Bard himself would, no doubt, have been astounded.

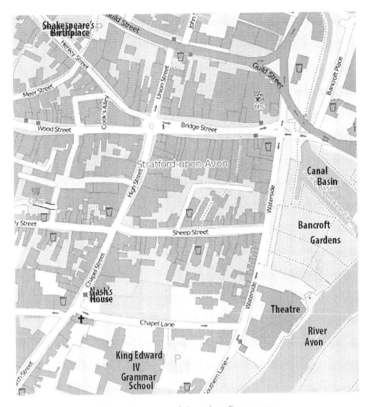

Map Courtesy of Creative Commons

The town itself is typically English midlands, which means it's almost always very busy with lots of shops and restaurants and, of course, people.

Bridge Street is the main street in Stratford. Not very historic, but a Mecca for shoppers; it runs all the way down to the river, and is a popular gathering place for visitors; there are a couple of nice pubs on Bridge Street, the Encore in particular. All the usual English shops are present, including Marks and Spencer, Boots the chemist/pharmacy, British Home Stores, Woolworth and so on. There are quaint little cafes, teashops, antique shops and souvenir shops and, of course, pubs.

Half-Timbered Shops in Stratford – Photo Courtesy of Creative Commons

Henley Street, one of Stratford's oldest streets, is a major tourist and shopping center. It's on Henley Street that you'll find Shakespeare's Birthplace, and the Shakespeare Centre, which was completed in 1964, is adjacent to Shakespeare's Birthplace.

Sheep Street runs from Ely Street and the Town Hall to Waterside and the Royal Shakespeare Theatre. Back in the 16th century, Sheep Street was a residential area.

As the name suggests, Sheep Street is where sheep, brought in from the nearby Cotswold Hills to be slaughtered, butchered and sold.

The Shrieves House on Sheep Street is one of the oldest houses in the town. Shakespeare, so the story goes, is supposed to have based his character Sir John Falstaff on one of its residents. To the rear of the Shrieves House is a museum, "Tudor World," which provides something of window into what life might have been like in the 16th century; it's well worth a visit. Just off Sheep Street,

16

Shrieves Walk is also worth a visit: small shops, cafes, boutiques etc.

Waterside runs from the foot of Bridge Street, along the banks of the River Avon to Holy Trinity Church and provides access to the church, the Royal Shakespeare Theatre, Bancroft Gardens and, of course, the river.

Waterside is very popular with locals and visitors alike. You can enjoy a picnic in Bancroft Gardens and all sorts of river-related activities: boat rides and tours, etc. In the summertime the River Avon is crowded with rowing boats, motor boats and river cruises.

Just about everything in Stratford is associated with the Bard. He looks down upon you in bronze from the top of the Gower Memorial in Bancroft Gardens, and from a half-a-hundred other places around the town.

The Gower Memorial in Bancroft Gardens – Photo Courtesy of Creative Commons

17

The Birmingham to Stratford Canal Basin, just off the Bancroft Gardens, is a busy gathering and mooring place for colorful narrow boats (the narrow boats are one-time coal or industrial barges that carted heavy goods along the canals, now converted into unique holiday/vacation homes). There are often jugglers, fire-eaters and magicians entertaining the public on the lawns. On the edge of the gardens there's a large fountain, the Swan Fountain, where the Stratford Town Walk meets every day (even Christmas Day), to offer a guided walking tour of the town; you should do the walk; it's a great way to learn all about the town and its history. The tour passes the Shakespeare houses, Royal Shakespeare Theatres, 15th century timber-framed buildings, William Shakespeare's school and visits Holy Trinity Church.

Narrow Boats Moored in the Canal Basin in Bancroft Gardens – Photo Courtesy of David Morris

Attractions:

One of the most popular attraction in Stratford, and only slightly less popular than Mr. Shakespeare himself, is the Royal Shakespeare Theatre, the home of the Royal Shakespeare Company and, one of Britain's most important cultural venues.

The Five Shakespeare Houses

Stratford's Shakespearian attractions also include five houses, all of which were a part of Shakespeare's life. All are now owned, operated and cared for by the Shakespeare Birthplace Trust. These include Hall's Croft (the one-time home of Shakespeare's daughter, Susanna, and her husband Dr. John Hall) and Nash's House, which stands alongside the site of another property, New Place, owned by Shakespeare himself, wherein he died. Anne Hathaway's Cottage, the home of Shakespeare's wife's family prior to her marriage, is in Shottery; Mary Arden's House, the family home of Shakespeare's mother, is about three miles outside of Stratford in Wilmscote. The five houses are covered in detail on the next page.

Then, of course, there's Holy Trinity Church on Waterside, where Shakespeare was baptized and is buried, and King Edward IV Grammar School on Church Street where Shakespeare is thought to have attended school, although no one knows for sure; the school is still in operation today.

The River Walk

I don't think I can ever remember a nicer experience than strolling along River Walk in Stratford on a Sunday afternoon in summer time. The word idyllic barely does this quiet and beautiful spot justice.

Photo Courtesy of David P. Howard .

The River Walk (above) as seen from Clopton Bridge. Even in late fall, when the trees are bare, this is the ideal spot for a quiet stroll.

The Five Shakespeare Houses

There are, as already mentioned, five houses in and around Stratford directly related to William Shakespeare, his family, and his life. All require that you pay an admittance fee. The most inexpensive way to do this is to purchase online at www.shakespeare.org.uk.

You can, if you prefer, purchase individual passes to each of the properties separately, but this is a much more expensive way to do it. I recommend you purchase a Five House Pass.

Shakespeare Five House Pass

The Five House Pass includes admission to Anne Hathaway's Cottage & Gardens, Hall's Croft, Mary Arden's

Farm, New Place & Nash's House, Shakespeare's Birthplace, and to Shakespeare's Grave which is actually located in Holy Trinity Church on Waterside. There is no admission fee to the church, but a donation is expected if you want to view the grave; the Five House Pass is accepted instead.

All tickets valid for 12 months (Mary Arden's Farm is open March through November) and cost:

Adult: £22.50

Child: £13.50

Family: £58.00

Shakespeare's Birthplace

William Shakespeare was born to John Shakespeare and Mary Arden in a half-timbered Tudor house on Henley Street in 1564. The house remains today much the same as it was in Elizabethan times. The living room has a flagstone floor, white walls, and oak beams. There is a large fireplace and many fine examples of furniture of the period. Upstairs you can view many of Shakespeare's original manuscripts, all written in old English script and flowing longhand.

Shakespeare's Birthplace on Henley Street – Photo Courtesy of Stuart
Yeates

The room in which Shakespeare was born has low ceilings and windows with leaden casements. There is a large oak bed, a wooden cradle, and a fine oak chest. The windows are covered with the signatures of such famous visitors as authors Thomas Carlyle and Sir Walter Scott.

The gardens that surround the house are beautiful indeed, and are said to contain at least one specimen of every flower, tree, and shrub mentioned in Shakespeare's plays.

John Shakespeare, Will's dad, purchased the dwelling in 1556; William was born there in 1564. The property remained in Shakespeare's family until 1670, when his granddaughter, Elizabeth Barnard, died. Elizabeth had no children, so the estate passed one of her relatives, Thomas Hart, and it remained in Hart's family for the rest of the 17th century.

The Gardens at the Rear of Shakespeare's Birthplace – Photo Courtesy of Grant Cherrington

Today, the property is owned, operated and cared for by the Shakespeare Birthplace Trust.

How to Get There:

Shakespeare's Birthplace is on Henley Street in downtown Stratford.

Admission:

Shakespeare Birthplace Pass provides admission to Shakespeare's Birthplace, Hall's Croft, New Place & Nash's House, and Shakespeare's Grave. This is the ideal if you only have a few hours

Adult: £14.95

Child: £9.00

Family: £38.50

Ann Hathaway's cottage is located just one mile down the road from Stratford in the tiny village of Shottery. Did you ever see anything more idyllic than this? It's hard to believe that such a chocolate box picture of a dwelling could exist outside of the movies, but it did, and it does.

Anne Hathaway's Cottage – Photo Courtesy of Tony Hisgett

The cottage is really a twelve room Elizabethan farm house. Ann married Shakespeare in 1582 and the cottage remained in the Hathaway family's possession until it was acquired by the Shakespeare trust in 1892.

The house contains lots of fine antique furniture, the most remarkable of which is Ann's Hathaway's bed. The rush mattress rests upon a support made from strands of rope; the exquisite needlework sheet is a Hathaway heirloom. In the living room, the great lady's early willow pattern dinner ware and pewter plates are displayed in a fine antique dresser.

The cottage, with its orchards and delightful country garden, is open to the public all year round.

Even when the snow is on the ground, Anne Hathaway's Cottage is a delight to behold – photo courtesy of Tony Hisgett.

How to Get There

Only about a mile-and-a-half outside of Stratford. Take the A422 Alcester road to Church Lane, turn left onto Church Lane and follow the signs.

Admission:

Your Shakespeare Five House Pass will work here. If you decide to purchase admission on-site, the fees are as follows:

Anne Hathaway's Cottage Ticket provides admission to the Cottage & Gardens

Adult: £9.00

Child: £5.00

Family: £22.50

Mary Arden's Home

Mary Arden's Farm, also known as Mary Arden's House, was thought to have been owned by Mary Shakespeare, the mother of William Shakespeare. The farm is located in the village of Wilmcote, about three miles outside of Stratford-upon-Avon. It was bought by the Shakespeare Birthplace Trust in 1930 and refurnished in the Tudor style.

The Palmer Farm – Photo Courtesy of Creative Commons

In 2000, however, it was discovered that it was not Mary Arden's house at all, but had belonged to her friend and neighbor, Adam Palmer; thus the house was renamed Palmer's Farm. The house that did actually belong to Mary Arden is located near to Palmer's Farm and was acquired by the Shakespeare Birthplace Trust in 1968.

The house and farm offer a tantalizing glimpse of what life might have been like in Tudor times, specifically 1573. Today, the farm is home to many rare breeds of animals including

26

Mangalitza and Tamworth Pigs, Cotswold Sheep, Long Horn Cattle, Baggot and Golden Guernsey Goats, Geese and assorted Birds of Prey including a Hooded Vulture.

The image above is Mary Arden's Farm –courtesy of Creative Commons.

How to Get There:

Mary Arden's farm is three and a half miles from the town centre in Wilmcote; take the A422 (Alcester Road) out of Stratford, turn right onto Ridgeway and then follow the signs: the site is well sign posted and free parking is provided on-site. Wilmcote railway station is a very short walk from the Farm.

Admission:

Note: The Farm is closed until 17 March 2014

Your Shakespeare Five House Pass will work here. If you decide to purchase admission on-site, the fees are as follows:

Adult: £9.95

Child: £6.50

Family: £26.50

Hall's Croft

Hall's Croft is a Tudor cottage that was owned by William Shakespeare's daughter, Susanna Hall and her husband Dr. John Hall whom she married in 1607.

Hall's Croft – Courtesy of Creative Commons

Today, the house contains a collection of 16th- and 17th-century paintings and furniture. There's also an exhibition about Doctor John Hall and the obscure medical practices of the period.

The property has a beautiful walled garden at the rear which contains a wide variety of plant life, including herbs that Dr. Hall is thought to have used in his treatments. The Halls later moved to New Place, which William Shakespeare left to his daughter after his death.

How to Get There:

Hall's Croft is on Old Town (Old Town is actually a street in Stratford); it's about a 10-minute walk from Shakespeare's Birthplace.

Admission:

Your Shakespeare Five House Pass will work here. If you decide to purchase admission on-site, the fees are as follows:

Adult: £14.95, Child: £9.00, Family: £38.50

Nash's House and New Place

Nash's House is the house located next door to the ruins and gardens of William Shakespeare's final residence, New Place. It has been converted into a museum that traces the history of Stratford-upon-Avon from the earliest settlers in the Avon Valley to Shakespeare's time.

New Place no longer exists. It stood on the corner of Chapel Street and Chapel Lane, and was apparently the second largest dwelling in the town. Now, only the beautiful gardens remain. New Place is accessible through the museum in Nash's House, which is the house next door.

The Knot Garden at New Place – Photo Courtesy of Creative Commons

The Great Garden at New Place – Photo Courtesy of Creative Commons

The Shakespeare Birthplace Trust acquired Nash's House and New Place in 1876.

How to Get There:

Nash's House and New Place are on Chapel Street, just a five-minute walk from Shakespeare's Birthplace.

Admission:

Your Shakespeare Five House Pass will work here. If you decide to purchase admission on-site, the fees are as follows:

Adult: £14.95, Child: £9.00, Family: £38.50

King Edward VI Grammar School

King Edward VI School in Stratford is, traditionally, a grammar school and academy for boys. Beginning in September of 2013, however, the school today does allow a limited number of girls to attend.

King Edward VI Grammar School– Courtesy of Creative Commons

31

There has been a school on this site since the early thirteenth century.

Tradition has it that William Shakespeare attended school here, but there is no real proof that he did. Circumstantially, however, the evidence suggests that he probably did attend the school: 1) Shakespeare certainly was well educated, are rare thing back in Tudor times; 2) As a child of Stratford upon Avon, William would have been entitled to a free place at the school; 3) there simply wasn't anywhere else for him to go to school. Therefore, it is likely that Shakespeare attended King Edward VI between the ages of seven and fourteen. His father, John Shakespeare, was an important man around Stratford in the mid-16th century: he was a glover (he made gloves) and wool dealer, and he was the bailiff of the borough in 1568.

How to Get There:

King Edward VI Grammar School is on Church Street, just a five-minute walk from Shakespeare's Birthplace.

Holy Trinity Church

Holy Trinity Church in Stratford-upon-Avon is, arguably, the most visited church in England, this is due to its fame as the place of baptism and burial of William Shakespeare.

The church is open to visitors pretty much the year-round, and each year it hosts more than 200,000 tourists.

Holy Trinity Church dates from 1210 and is built on the site of a Saxon monastery on the banks of the River Avon.

Holy Trinity Church in Stratford-upon-Avon - Photo Courtesy of
Lindsey Dearing

Shakespeare, poet and playwright, was baptized in Holy
Trinity on 26 April 1564 and was buried there on 25 April 1616.
The original Elizabethan register giving details of his baptism is
held by the Shakespeare Birthplace Trust for safekeeping.

Shakespeare is buried in the beautiful 15th-century chancel
built by Thomas Balsall, Dean of the Collegiate Church, who
was also buried there in 1491. Shakespeare's funerary monument
is fixed on a wall alongside his burial place.

Shakespeare's wife Anne Hathaway is buried next to him
along with his eldest daughter Susanna.

Shakespeare Funerary Monument – Photo Courtesy of Creative Commons

Above Shakespeare's grave, a badly eroded stone slab displays his epitaph:

GOOD FRIEND FOR JESUS SAKE FOREBEAR,

TO DIGG THE DVST ENCLOSED HERE.

BLESTE BE YE MAN YT SPARES THESE STONES,

AND CURSED BE HE YT MOVES MY BONES.

Legend has it that the warning has served to prevent both the removal of Shakespeare's body to Westminster Abbey, and the exhumation of his body for examination.

Shakespeare's Grave – Photo Courtesy of Creative Commons

Anne Hathaway is next to her husband's (at left in the photo). The inscription on her stone states, "Here lyeth the body of Anne wife of William Shakespeare who departed this life the 6th day of August 1623 being of the age of 67 years."

How to Get There:

Holy Trinity Church is on Old Town, less than a 10-minute walk from Shakespeare's Birthplace.

Admission:

A small donation is requested to access the chancel and sanctuary where Shakespeare and members of his family are buried (Your Shakespeare Five House Pass will do instead).

Your Shakespeare Five House Pass will work here.

The Royal Shakespeare Theatre

Last, but not least, we come to the Royal Shakespeare Theatre; no visit to Stratford would be complete without spending a few moments, if only in the gardens that surround it.

I have lost count of the number of times I have visited the RST. I have seen almost all of Shakespeare's plays, some of them more than once. I have seen the Merry Wives of Windsor twice and the Henry V three times. It's an experience you won't soon forget.

Photo Courtesy of Creative Commons

As we already know, the Royal Shakespeare Theatre is one of the most popular of Stratford's attractions, but here's the thing: Although Shakespeare was born in Stratford 1564, and died in 1616 at the age of 51, none of his plays were professionally performed in Stratford until more than 150 years later in 1769 when the first real theater in Stratford was built by the actor David Garrick for his Shakespeare Jubilee celebrations of that year to mark Shakespeare's birthday; and even that was no more than a temporary wooden structure. Garrick's theatre was built on a site not far from that of the present Royal Shakespeare Theatre.

Next, it was the turn of one Charles Edward Flower, a local brewer to jump into the theater business. His theater, also a temporary wooden structure, was built in 1864 to celebrate the 300th anniversary of Shakespeare's birth.

Known as the Tercentenary Theatre, it was built in a section of the brewer's large gardens on what is today the site of the Courtyard Theatre, now closed. The Tercentenary Theatre lasted only for three months before it was dismantled. But the erstwhile Mr. Flowers was not yet finished. In the early 1870s, he donated several acres along the riverside to the local council on the understanding that a permanent theatre would be built in honor of Shakespeare's memory, and by 1879 the first Shakespeare Memorial Theatre had been completed. Unfortunately, that theater was destroyed by fire in 1926.

And so we come almost to the present day, well... 1932, when English architect Elisabeth Scott, created the theater we have today. The adjoining Swan Theatre was created in the 1980s out of the shell of the remained of the original Shakespeare Memorial Theatre.

Photo Courtesy of Creative Commons

You really should try to spend some time at RST; you don't have to watch a play if you don't want to, but the food in the Rooftop restaurant on the third floor of the theatre is the finest, and that's not to mention the stunning views over the river Avon below. If you do decide to see a play, you can enjoy such works as: Twelfth Night, Henry V, The Merry Wives of Windsor, and A Midsummer Night's Dream, as they are acted out by the members of the Royal Shakespeare Company.

Photo Courtesy of Creative Commons

Before leaving Stratford you should take the time to wander through the gardens that surround the theatre, stroll along the riverbank, or linger for a moment by the Shakespeare Memorial and read the inscriptions on the statues of Hamlet, Falstaff, Prince Henry, Lady Macbeth, and Shakespeare himself.

Where to Stay

There are many fine hotels in Stratford-upon-Avon, and one can usually find something to fit the budget. The tourist season is always heavy so be sure to book your hotel well in advance. The English bed-and-breakfast is probably the best value for your money. Because so many people open their houses to the public, you don't have to book this type of accommodation in advance.

Bed & Breakfast

Gowers Close B&B

Gowers Close is a picture-book thatched cottage set in the charming village of Sibford Gower in the Northeast Cotswolds with large windows that provide stunning views of the cottage gardens. It's about 18 miles from Stratford, and I include it here because it's a very lovely drive from the village into Stratford, and because it's within easy reach of the Cotswolds, should you desire to visit.

Not a large B&B: just two lovely guestrooms - one king sized double and one twin - both with private bathrooms, garden views, and tea and coffee making facilities.

So, if you're looking for somewhere special to stay, a relaxing weekend, long country walks, and hospitality you'll talk about for years to come, Gowers Close is exactly what you're looking for.

Gowers Close is in Sibford Gower some 18 miles from Stratford and 14 miles from Chipping Campden, about 3/4 mile south of the B4035 between Banbury and Chipping Campden, and about 7 miles west of M40 (Exit 11).

Double occupancy is from £70.00 per night. Single occupancy £50.00.

40

Contact: Judith Hitching and John Marshall GOWERS CLOSE, Sibford Gower, Oxfordshire. OX15 5RW; Phone 01295 780348; Email: judith@gowersclose.co.uk

Ambleside Guesthouse

Ambleside Guesthouse is a nice little B&B set in the heart of Stratford. Ambleside offers a choice of seven very comfortable guest rooms, some with private bath; all have TVs, tea and coffee making facilities, ironing facilities, and hairdryers. Double, single and family rooms are available and breakfast is, of course, included in the rate.

Ambleside is centrally located and is less than a 5 minute walk from Downtown Stratford and the Royal Shakespeare and Swan Theatres.

Ambleside Guesthouse is a non-smoking facility and does not take in children under the age of 7.

Rates:

Expect to pay between £40 and £80 per night, depending upon the room.

Contact:

Ambleside Guesthouse, 41 Grove Road, Stratford-upon-Avon, Warks. CV37 6PB; Telephone 01789 297239; eMail peter@amblesideguesthouse.com

Moonraker Guesthouse

The Moonraker Guest House is "a traditional English 4 star-rated guest house with excellent en-suite rooms (private bathrooms), delicious home cooking, friendly service and a cozy atmosphere."

All rooms have private shower/bath rooms, TVs, hairdryer, clock radio, tea and coffee making facilities. Moonraker is a non-smoking accommodation with free parking available in allocated parking spaces. Internet is available only in the guest's lounge.

Okay, so that's the official stuff, but what is it really like? First, Moonraker is ideally placed on the Alcester Road. If you want, it's close enough to be able to walk into town, or even to Anne Hathaway's Cottage. Some of the rooms are a bit cramped for space, but not uncomfortably so; the facilities, both/showers etc., are clean and appealing. The breakfast? Good, not over the top, but properly cooked and pleasantly served.

Then, there are the landlords: Morris and Ruth. Morris is one of those rare people that can make friends with just about anybody. He's charming, friendly and eager to help; nothing is too much trouble for him.

Moonraker is good value for the money.

Rates:

Expect to pay upward of £45 per night for a single room, and from £70 per night for a double room - the rate includes breakfast.

Contact:

Moonraker Guest House, 40 Alcester Road, Stratford-upon-Avon, Warwickshire. CV37 9DB; Telephone 01789 268774;eMail info@moonrakerhouse.com

Hotels

Ettington Park Hotel

The Ettington Park Hotel is the only AA 4-Red Star hotel in Stratford upon Avon. Set on more than 40 acres of pristine and beautifully landscaped gardens and parkland, Ettington Park is a hotel in the grand manor.

Situated just six miles from the Stratford town center, with easy access to the Cotswolds, "this spectacular Neo-Gothic mansion is a world apart from the hustle and bustle of modern-day life." Ettington Park is a Handpicked Hotel.

So, if you want to live for a couple of days in the "grand manor," I suggest you consider Ettington Park.

Rates:

Expect to pay from $105 per night per double room.

Contact:

Ettington Park Hotel, Alderminster, Stratford-upon-Avon, Warwickshire, CV37 8BU; Phone 0845 072 7454; eMail ettingtonpark@handpicked.co.uk

Salford Hall

I can't believe they have turned Salford Hall into a Best West Western hotel, but so they have, and that is a very good thing. I could not recount the number of fines times and dinners I have enjoyed at Salford Hall; my step father had one of his receptions there when he was mayor of Evesham. Be that as it may, Salford Hall would make a great venue for your stay in Shakespeare Country and as a jumping off point for all things Shakespeare.

Salford Hall is a Tudor manor house that looks almost as if time has forgotten it, but it hasn't. The photo above is courtesy of Dave Bushell.

The Grade 1 listed property has lovingly been restored and outfitted with all the modern conveniences we 21st century travelers have come to expect. Having said that, if you want to get a glimpse of what it was like to live in Tudor England, this is the place to do it. Many of the 36 guest rooms have low, beamed ceilings - some even have fireplaces and four-poster beds; all have private bathrooms and all of the little incidentals and toiletries that the Best Western chain offers world-wide.

The public rooms feature inglenook fireplaces, oak beams and wood paneling. Best of all, the hotel is only eight miles from Stratford, and there's plenty of free parking on the grounds.

Rates: Expect to pay around 75 per night, including breakfast.

Contact:

BEST WESTERN Salford Hall Hotel, Abbots Salford, Stratford upon Avon, Warwickshire, WR11 8UT; Telephone 01386 871300The Swan's Nest Hotel

Alveston Manor Hotel

The Alveston Manor Hotel and Spa is just a 5 minute' walk from downtown Stratford-upon-Avon. The hotel, a historic Tudor manor house, is surrounded by beautifully landscaped gardens and is one of the finest 4-star hotels in Shakespeare Country.

Photo Courtesy of Dave Skinner

With 113 guest rooms, the Alveston Manor is quite a large hotel, considering where it is, with plenty of free parking (always a big consideration, especially as the hotel is as close as it is to the theater and downtown attractions). The hotel also offers extensive meeting rooms making it ideal for corporate travelers. Free WiFi is also available in all public and guest rooms. Guestrooms all have air-conditioning, flat screen televisions, private bathrooms, and all the little niceties you would expect to find in a modern luxury hotel.

Rates:

Expect to pay from £95 per person per night (includes breakfast).

Contact:

Macdonald Alveston Manor Hotel, Clopton Bridge, Stratford-upon-Avon, CV37 7HP, GB; Telephone 844 879 9138

Welcombe Hotel

This another hotel I am very familiar with and, I have to say, one of my favorites, and not just because of the golf course. If you're looking for a four star hotel in Stratford-upon-Avon, the Welcombe Hotel Spa & Golf Club offers the ultimate English country house retreat.

Not as old as some of its peers, the Welcombe dates to 1866 and is set in more than 150 acres of beautiful, landscaped gardens. An English, Jacobean-style house that offers an old-world experience, including luxurious suites with four-poster beds. The hotel also offers fine dining, a luxury spa, private bathrooms, flat screen TVs and free WiFi, and every other modern convenience in all of the guest rooms.

The Welcombe Hotel – Photo Courtesy of Creative Commons

If you play golf, you should try the 18-hole layout at the hotel: a par 70 tract that plays some 6,288 yards from the back tees.

Then there is the Spa: The Spa facilities, which are free to hotel residents, include an impressive indoor swimming pool, a separate external vitality pool, heated loungers and foot spas. Treatments run from £55.00 for a 30 minute back, neck and shoulder massage, and up from there.

I can personally recommend the Welcombe, having visited the place many times, both as a guest and for dinner. The rooms are spacious and clean, the spa facilities are also very clean, and they compare favorably with any spa I have ever visited anywhere in the world (and I have visited a lot of spa over the years).

On the downside, and this is really all I could come up with: the parking on-site is a little limited, and the restaurant is expensive. All-in-all, though, you get what you pay for: a very nice, 4-star experience.

47

Rates:

Expect to pay from £108 to £195 per night, depending upon the day of the week, the room and the time of year.

Contact:

Menzies Welcombe Hotel Spa and Golf Club, Warwick Road, Stratford-upon-Avon, Warwickshire, CV37 0NR;   Tel: 01789   29525;   Email: welcombe@menzieshotels.co.uk

Where to Eat in Stratford

As we all know, restaurants come and go, seemingly with the seasons. That being so, it makes no sense to offer up a never-ending list of places to eat. If I did, this book would be out of date before I finished writing it. Instead, I will provide you with just a few that have been around for a long time, and that I know personally.

Stratford does have many fine restaurants, both downtown and out of town. There are also plenty of fast food restaurants, including Pizza Hut, McDonalds, Domino's Pizza and a whole lot more: you certainly won't starve in Stratford.

For dinner, you could do no better than visit:

The Dirty Duck

The Garrick Inn

The Royal Shakespeare Theater

The Welcombe Hotel

The Salford Hall

The Arden Hotel

All of the above are covered in some detail either in the Where to Stay section, or in the Good Pubs section.

Or you can choose from any one of a half-a-hundred taverns and inns that specialize in the local fair: shepherd's pie, plowman's lunch, or good sandwiches made to your order

There is, however, one other great place to eat dinner I will mention particularly, and I do so because I have many fond memories of the restaurant and I highly recommend it:

The Arrow Mill at Alcester

Arrow Mill Hotel & Restaurant is located less than ten miles (a short, 15-minute drive) from Stratford upon Avon on the banks of the River Arrow. The setting is spectacular, the food is beyond compare, and the atmosphere is friendly and inviting. You will need to make a reservation: Phone 01789 762419

How to Get There

Take the A46 Alcester Road to Alcester, then the A422 to the 1st exit, then left and drive to the Mill.

Good Pubs in Stratford

There are one or two nice pubs in Stratford I can share with you:

The Dirty Duck

The Dirty Duck is located on the waterside not far from the Swan Theater on Southern Lane, and just a short walk from the town center. The pub used to be called the Black Swan, but the American soldiers that were camped on the other side of the river during World War II affectionately called it the Dirty Duck, and the name stuck.

The Dirty Duck Pub on Waterside – Photo Courtesy of Lindsey Dearing

Today, the Dirty Duck serves a great pint of beer and good food too. Pub food, here and almost everywhere, is not what it once was. Most old-world pubs have been transformed into restaurants; the Dirty Duck is no exception. The menu at the Dirty Duck is extensive and a mish-mash of cuisine from an assortment of cultures, including Indian, Italian, English traditional food (steaks, chicken, etc.) along with one or two pub-style dishes (sausage and mash, fish and chips). Be that as it may, the beer is good and food more than just acceptable.

The Garrick Inn

The Garrick is the oldest pup in Stratford, a 15th century timber framed building rich in history and atmosphere and is, so they say, haunted by many a lost soul. Be that as it may, it's a nice place to eat and the beer is good too. Unfortunately, the bar is rather small and can become quite crowded. Go early in the evening.

The Garrick Inn on High Street – Photo Courtesy of Tony Hisgett

I have visited the Garrick on a number of occasions and I've never had a bad experience.

The service is good, the staff is friendly, and the prices are reasonable, at least for Stratford. It really is a place to eat rather than to hang out. The curry is a good choice at £7.95, which includes a drink, and the traditional roast beef with Yorkshire pudding is also a good choice at £8.99

The Garrick Inn is on High Street next to the town hall.

The Windmill Inn

The Windmill Inn is another old-world pub in Stratford dating back to the 16th Century. It's located on Church Street, not far from the Shakespeare's birthplace.

The Flower's beer is excellent. The Windmill is a nice place to each lunch. They offer a range of home-style sandwiches, and tea or coffee is you prefer it.

The Windmill Inn on Church Street – Photo Courtesy of Creative Commons

How to Get to Stratford

Stratford-upon-Avon is easy to get to by train, bus and by road: Assuming that you'll be arriving in England via one of London's airports, and that you'll be traveling to Shakespeare country from there, either for the day, or for a longer stay, there are several travel options you might like to consider. Me? I always go by road, but the train is cheaper, often easier, and certainly more scenic.

By Road

Stratford-upon-Avon is roughly 100 miles northwest of London via the M4, M25. M40 and A46 roads. It's a drive of about 2 hours 15 minutes to drive. Take the M40 north to junction 15 - the A429/A46 (Stratford Road) and dive on into Stratford; it's motorway driving almost all of the way so it's an easy run. Keep in mind that gasoline, called petrol in the UK, is very expensive (about $5 per gallon) and sold by the liter (a little more than a quart).

By Train

One of the best, and the cheapest, ways to get to Stratford is by train. Trains leave from London Marylebone Station about every two hours – up to five times per day in each direction, and up to seven times per day from London to Stratford. The trip takes 2 hours 15 minutes, with round trip advance fares starting about £10. Stratford Parkway railway station is located just to the north of the town within easy reach of the hotels via taxi.

Visit by Guided Tour

Premier Tours out of London offer several guided tours to Shakespeare Country. Go to premiertours.co.uk, or you get information and book your tour by telephone; in the UK, call 020 7713 1311; in the U.S., call 1-800-815-4003. These folks offer a full range of guide tours including the Cotswolds (£69), Stonehenge (£80) and, of course, Shakespeare Country including Stratford (£80), and Warwick Castle (£73). As always, prices are subject to change without notice.

Warwick and Kenilworth

Kenilworth and Warwick are two historic towns located just a few miles to the northeast of Stratford-upon-Avon. Each has a magnificent castle. You could easily visit both in a single day.

Warwick

Warwick is the county town of Warwickshire located about nine miles from Stratford-upon-Avon. Warwick is a small community of about 35,000 people with one or two interesting Tudor buildings, a university, an amazing church, a horse racing course and one of the most important castles in England.

View over Warwick with the Church of St. Mary in the Background – Photo Courtesy of Creative Commons

There has been a settlement of one sort or another at Warwick for more than 2,000 years. The great Saxon lady, Ethelfleda, Lady of the Mercians and daughter of King Alfred the Great, built a fortified dwelling, or burh, at Warwick early in the 10th century.

Warwick Castle was established just after the Norman Conquest of 1066. In those early times it was little more than a wooden stockade with a central keep, not quite the vast structure we see today.

Warwick Castle as Seen from the Church of St. Mary – Photo Courtesy of Paul Englefield

In 1088, King William created the earldom of Warwick and the castle became the home of the earls of Warwick, and remained so until the 1970s. The earls of Warwick became very influential in the development of England.

Today, very little of medieval Warwick remains. Most of the Tudor structures were destroyed by fire in 1694, so most of the buildings post-date this period. Of the medieval buildings that do remain, the most significant are the Lord Leycester Hospital which dates to the late 14th century, and the Church of St. Mary, also 14th century, but set on 12th century foundations.

The Lord Leycester Hospital - known simply as the Lord Leycester - is now a retirement home for ex-Servicemen, retired members of the military; the old hospital is located next to the West Gate, on High Street.

The Lord Leycester Hospital on High Street in Warwick – Photo Courtesy of Creative Commons

The Hospital includes the medieval Chapel of St James the Great; the living quarters include the Master's House, dining and reception rooms, a Guildhall, several anterooms and a Great Hall. The property also includes the Master's Garden and the Museum of the Queen's Own Hussars.

The Chapel of St James was built in 1126 by Roger de Newburgh, the 2nd Earl of Warwick. In the late 14th century, however, it was rebuilt by the 12th Earl of Warwick. The Guildhall was built in 1450 by the 16th Earl of Warwick.

The Lord Leycester Hospital on High Street in Warwick – Photo
Courtesy of Tony Grist

The 1st Earl of Leicester, Robert Dudley, acquired the buildings in 1571 and, under royal charter from Queen Elizabeth I, he founded therein a hospital for aged or injured soldiers and their wives. The hospital was run by 12 resident "Brethren" (originally soldiers) under the charge of a "Master", and was funded from the income of various estates.

In 1956 the Corporation of the Master and Brethren of the Hospital was abolished by an Act of Parliament and was replaced with a board of Governors. During the mid-1960s, the old hospital underwent an extensive restoration.

The hospital reopened in 1966. Today, the hospital is run by the Master, a retired officer of the Armed Forces, and is home to eight ex-servicemen and their wives.

Warwick Castle

Warwick Castle is an imposing fortress set on a sandstone bluff above the town of Warwick, at a bend of the River Avon which runs below the castle on its east side. The river has eroded the rock the castle stands on, forming a cliff. The river and cliff form natural defenses for the great castle.

Warwick Castle – Photo Courtesy of David Stowell

Warwick castle was built in 1068 by William the Conqueror to maintain control of the Midlands as he advanced northwards following the initial invasion of England in 1066

The original structure was a motte-and-bailey structure. This form of castle was the traditional Norman design and consisted of a large mound or hill upon which the keep or tower stood; the keep was surrounded by a curtain wall, the bailey, which an enclosed a courtyard which could provide refuge to the townspeople and homes for the castle garrison and servants.

In the early days, the curtain wall, and much of the castle itself, would have been made of wood; it would have been more a stockade than castle. That, however, did not last for long. Slowly, the great stone castle we see today replaced the old wooden fortress.

Warwick Castle – Photo Courtesy of Creative Commons

From 1088, when King William invested Henry de Beaumont as the first Earl of Warwick, Warwick castle has been home to the earls for almost 900 years. The history of the castle is significant, extensive and far too in-depth to describe here.

It will take you at least half a day to tour the public rooms, galleries, and gardens of the castle. Of special interest is the great hall, the largest room in the castle. It was built in the 14th century and was the place where most of the castle activity took place.

The castle is unique because it is almost intact, having served as the home of the Earls of Warwick until the 8th Earl sold it to Madame Tussauds in 1978 (the numbering seems to have started over in the 16th century – Richard Neville 1449-1471 was the 16th earl. Then came two more Plantagenet earls, George and Edward. The Plantagenet line of earls ended when Henry VII won the Wars of the Roses. John Dudley was created the new 1st Earl of Warwick in 1504, and the line continued through the 8th Earl who sold the castle in 1978).

If you climb the steps to the top of the towers, you can gaze out over the countryside and imagine what brave deeds of chivalry must have taken place in the fields below.

Commons and Warwick Castle – Photo Courtesy of Bently Photography

The castle gardens are believed to be the first works of the great English gardener, Capability Brown. After you have wandered among the peacocks and taken the grand tour of the conservatory, you can take lunch or afternoon tea in the castle restaurant.

You will certainly want to visit the castle dungeon with its fine collection of instruments of torture. And you will wonder how anyone could have survived a stay in the "oubliette," a tiny dungeon within a dungeon.

The Great Hall at Warwick Castle – Photo Courtesy of Creative Commons

The Great Hall is full of historical memorabilia. There's a fine collection of arms, including a full set of equestrian armor; the rider is outfitted for jousting.

Warwick Castle – Photo Courtesy of Martin Addison

Opening Hours:

Warwick castle is open to the public all year round from 10am until 5.30 pm.

Admission:

Adult   £25.80

Child   £19.80

Senior   £21.60

Family of 4   £90.00

Family of 5   £109.20

Book your tickets at warwick-castle.com and save up to 20%.

St Mary is a Church of England parish church located close the town center in Warwick, just east of the market place. Although most of the church you see today dates only to 1704, St. Mary's beginnings date back almost 900 years to just after the Norman Conquest. Roger de Beaumont, 2nd Earl of Warwick, caused the construction of St. Mary in 1123, and at the same time founded the College of Dean and Canons at the church. The only surviving part of the Norman church which de Beaumont built is the crypt. The chancel vestries and chapter house of the church were extensively rebuilt in the 14th century by the 11th Earl of Warwick, Thomas de Beauchamp.

The Collegiate Church of St. Mary – Photo Courtesy of Creative Commons

Thomas was quite a character, and a brilliant military commander: he commanded the English army against the Scotts in 1337, and part of the army against the French at both Crecy and Poitiers, both were huge victories for the Black Prince; Okay, back to St. Mary's Church.

The Interior of St. Mary's Church – Photo Courtesy of Creative Commons

Thomas de Beauchamp's descendants built the Chapel of Our Lady, commonly known as the Beauchamp Chapel. (By the way, it is pronounced Beecham). The chapel is worth a visit, because it contains monuments to Richard de Beauchamp, 13th Earl of Warwick, Ambrose Dudley, 3rd

Earl of Warwick, and Robert Dudley, 1st Earl of Leicester. Robert Dudley was a favorite of Queen Elizabeth I.

The Beauchamp Chapel – Photo Courtesy of Creative Commons

Robert Dudley and his wife Lettice – Courtesy of Creative Commons

The nave and tower of Beauchamp's church, along with much of Warwick itself, were completely destroyed in the Great Fire of Warwick of 1694. The church was rebuilt in 1704 in the Gothic style by William Wilson. The tower rises to the height of 130 feet and is prominent landmark on the Warwick skyline.

Best Pubs in Warwick

The Tudor House Inn

The Tudor House Inn on West Street, just across the street from Warwick Castle, is an authentic oak beamed 15th century building (1472) serving "Real Ales" and good food. If you visit the castle, you can't miss it; it's one of the most recognized of the few medieval buildings that survived the Great Fire of Warwick of 1694.

Interesting is a word that does not do justice to this Medieval hotel. The ceilings are low and feature heavy oak beams, the stairs are steep and narrow and the rooms are small. The inn has ten guest rooms, eight of which have private bathrooms; all are equipped with tea/coffee makers and TVs; Iron and Ironing board and hairdryers are available on request; free Wi-Fi is also available. Single, double and family rooms are available. Parking can be a bit of problem (two hours on the street)

The food is very good, especially the breakfast. The staff are very friendly and ever-ready to help; the Inn is just a two-minute walk from downtown Warwick. Bed and Breakfast is available, but be sure to book in plenty of time before you visit Warwick.

Contact:

The Tudor House Inn, 90 - 92 West Street, Warwick, England, CV34 6AW. Phone 1926 495447.

The Rose and Crown

The Rose and Crown is a typical English pub set on the corner of Market Street in Warwick.

Photo Courtesy of Kenneth Allen

67

There are not many pubs that I frequent when I'm in in Warwick, but the Rose and Crown is one of them. It's a favorite with locals and visitors alike. The beer is excellent, and the food is even better.

Food is available throughout the day, including breakfast and a full menu for lunch and dinner. For visitors to Warwick, the Rose and Crown is just the place to enjoy a good lunch. The Rose and Crown has won several national awards, including being named twice to the Top Ten UK pubs and the Best Pub in the UK in 2004.

Expect to pay between £7 and £12 per person for lunch (does not include a drink) and between £13.50 and £35.00 for dinner.

Bed and Breakfast is available too: The Rose & Crown is featured in the current Alastair Sawday's Special Places – Pubs & Inns Guide, and also appears as a "pub worth visiting" in The Good Pub Guide 2014. The Rose and Crown has 13 guest rooms, five of which are located directly over the pub with eight more in a separate building.

All have private bathrooms along with all the usual facilities: TVs, etc. Double rooms, family rooms, twins and singles are available.

Contact:

Rose & Crown, 30 Market Place, Warwick CV34 4SH, United Kingdom; Telephone +44 1926 411117

The New Bowling Green

The New Bowling Green on St. Nicholas Church Street is a neat little 15th century, Tudor style pub with a large, walled beer garden backing onto St Nicholas Park. The pub offers a selection of home cooked food, which is available daily between 12 noon and 4pm; the beer is good too. The New Bowling Green is handily placed on St. Nicholas Church Street just a short walk from Warwick Castle's main gate. I have visited this pub several times and I have always enjoyed the experience, hence its inclusion here.

Photo Courtesy of the New Bowling Green

Contact:

New Bowling Green, 13 St Nicholas Church Street, Warwick, CV34 4JD, UK; Telephone 01926 411470

How to Get to Warwick:

Warwick is a short 9-mile drive from Stratford; take the A439 Warwick Road out of Stratford. It's a drive of about 20 minutes, depending upon the traffic.

Kenilworth

Kenilworth approximately 4 miles north of Warwick and 14 miles north of Stratford upon Avon. Other than the extensive ruins of Kenilworth Castle, the ruins of Kenilworth Abbey in Abbey Fields Park, St Nicholas' Parish Church and the Kenilworth Clock in the Warwick Road, there's not much more to see.

It seems there must have been a settlement of some sort, probably a Saxon farm, on the site of Kenilworth even before Geoffrey de Clinton built his castle and priory in 1124.

Kenilworth Castle

When I visit Kenilworth I try to do it early in the morning. There is nothing quite like watching the sunrise over the castle ruins.

History has seen many notable owners of Kenilworth castle: Geoffrey de Clinton in 1122, John of Gaunt in the

1350s, then the Earl of Leicester in 1563, and finally the Duke of Clarendon who gave it to the nation in 1958.

Geoffrey de Clinton founded his castle at Kenilworth in 1122 around a great tower, construction would continue over several centuries. King John enlarged it extensively at the beginning of the 13th century.

Model of Kenilworth Castle - Courtesy of Creative Commons

Huge water defenses were created by damming the local streams and the resulting fortifications proved able to withstand assaults by land and water in 1266.

Photo Courtesy of Paul Johnson

John of Gaunt in the mid-14th century continued the expansion, turning the medieval castle into a palace fortress. Robert Dudley, the Earl of Leicester and Queen Elizabeth 1st's favorite, then expanded the castle once again, constructing new Tudor buildings and turned the great fortress into a fashionable palace.

Leicester's Gate House - Courtesy Creative Commons & David Stowell

Dudley built the inner court of the castle in the 1570s. He also built a tower now known as Leicester's building on the south edge of the court as a guest wing, extending out beyond the inner bailey wall for extra space.

Leicester's building was four floors high and built in a fashionable, contemporary Tudor style with "brittle, thin walls and grids of windows". The building was intended to appear well-proportioned alongside the ancient great tower, one of the reasons for its considerable height.

The Ancient Tower or Keep - Courtesy Creative Commons

Throughout English history, Kenilworth has played an important historical role. The castle was the subject of the six-month long Siege of Kenilworth in 1266, believed to be the longest siege in English history, and was a base for the Lancastrian forces during the Wars of the Roses.

The Great Hall - Courtesy Creative Commons

Kenilworth castle was also the scene of the removal of Edward II from the English throne, and Robert Dudley's lavish reception for Queen Elizabeth I in 1575.

Kenilworth castle was partly destroyed by the Parliamentary forces commanded by Oliver Cromwell in 1649 to prevent it from ever being used again as a military stronghold. Today, only two of the castle buildings are habitable. The present ruins include Mortimer's Tower, Leicester's Gate-House, the Great Keep, the Great Hall, and the state apartments.

Opening Hours:

English Heritage has managed the castle since 1984. The castle is open to visitors on weekdays all year round from 9.30 am until 5.30 pm and on Sundays 2pm until 5.30.

Admission:

Member of English Heritage: Free (you can join online- the passes are good for all English Heritage sites.

Adult: £9.00; Child (5-15 years): £5.40; Family (2 adults, 3 children):£23.40;

Overseas Visitor Pass are available

St. Mary's Abbey Kenilworth

St. Mary's Abbey at Kenilworth came into being in 1124 as a priory built for the Augustinians by Geoffrey de Clinton at around the same time he began the construction of Kenilworth Castle. St Nicholas' Church was built in the abbey gardens in about 1291. The priory was designated an abbey by Pope Nicholas V in 1447. The abbey fell victim to King Henry VIII and the Dissolution of the Monasteries and was dismantled sometime after 1538.

The Abbey Gate - Courtesy Creative Commons

Today, all that remains of the once great abbey are few ruins (most of them underground), the gatehouse and the barn. The ruins were excavated in 1840, 1880 and 1922; most of the ruins were covered in 1967 for their protection.

The Abbey Cloisters - Courtesy Creative Commons

The remains of St Mary's Abbey are located in the grounds of St Nicholas' Church and in an adjacent area of Abbey Fields.

St. Nicholas' Church

St. Nicholas is a fine example of a 14th century, Perpendicular-style English parish church, with Tudor alterations. The church is was constructed using the same red sandstone used to build Kenilworth castle. It sits right beside the Norman and medieval ruins of St Mary's Abbey.

St. Nicholas' Church Kenilworth - Courtesy Creative Commons

Kenilworth's parish church, where Queen Elizabeth I worshipped when she was a guest of Robert Dudley, Lord Leicester. Elizabeth was a frequent visitor at Kenilworth: in 1566, 1568, 1572 and again in 1575 when she stayed at the castle for an extended period. During that stay, she attended Holy Communion at St Nicholas' Church three times. The church still owns and uses the silver chalice from which Elizabeth was given communion on these occasions.

St Nicholas' Church is located about a half-mile from the castle, an easy ten-minute walk, just off High Street in Kenilworth.

How to Get to Kenilworth

Take the A46 north out of Warwick to its junction with the A452, turn left and the follow the road into Kenilworth; it's a drive of about 5 miles.

Stoneleigh and Stoneleigh Abbey

Stoneleigh Village

Stoneleigh is a small village in Warwickshire on the banks of River Sowe. It's about three miles from Kenilworth. So, while you're visiting Kenilworth and its castle, it makes sense to stop in here as well.

Stoneleigh is a tiny community on the river, very pretty, and one of those beautiful spots we all love to visit. Be sure to stop ind visit the Stoneleigh village church, the Church of the Virgin Mary.

Stoneleigh Village - Photo Courtesy of Creative Commons

Church of the Virgin Mary, Stoneleigh - Photo Courtesy of Creative Commons

Best Pubs:

Stoneleigh does not have a pub. It did. In fact, it once had three. The story has it that they were all closed by Lord Leigh more than 100 years ago, after his daughter was laughed at by drunks when she was going to church on a tricycle.

How to Get There:

Take Dalehouse Lane out of Kenilworth and drive to Stonleigh Road and then follow the signs; it's a short drive of about three miles.

Stoneleigh Abbey

Stoneleigh Abbey is a large country mansion situated just to the southwest of the village. The original Abbey was founded by the Cistercians in 1154 but, following the Dissolution of the Monasteries during the reign of King

Henry VIII, very little remains of the original Abbey buildings, the 14th century Gatehouse.

Following the Dissolution of the Monasteries, the estate was acquired by Sir Thomas Leigh, Lord Mayor of London in 1558, and a house was built - the north and west wings of the present house - on the site of the monastic buildings.

Between the years 1714 and 1726 a new four story, fifteen bay west wing designed by architect Francis Smith was added and it includes the State apartments. The great house was the home of the Leigh family from 1561 to 1990.

In 1996 Lord Leigh transferred the ownership of the Abbey to a charitable trust. Between 1996 and 2000 the Abbey underwent extensive renovations.

Stoneleigh Abbey - Photo Courtesy of Creative Commons

Stoneleigh Abbey is open from Good Friday to 31st October on Tuesdays, Wednesdays, Thursdays, and

Sundays. Stoneleigh Abbey is also open on Bank Holidays. The grounds are open from 11 AM until 5PM on opening days. The house is open by guided tour only. Tours last just over an hour and run throughout the day.

Shakespeare's Towns and Villages

The towns and villages of Shakespeare Country are little changed from what they must have been like when the bard walked the woods and pathways of this beautiful countryside. If this is your first visit, I envy you, you are in for a rare treat.

The ideal way to visit is via the back roads for a scenic, leisurely drive and explore the market towns and villages. Along the way you can stop, take photos, hike a short way along the numerous footpaths, and enjoy traditional ales and home cooked food in one or more of the many country pubs.

This is where we explore, not only Shakespeare's country but, at least in my opinion, God's country too. I have put together several driving tours that will take you deep into the heart of Shakespeare country. All can be done in a single day, but you can combine any or all of them if you wish, and stop off for the night at one of the bed and breakfast inns or pubs I have listed for you.

You'll visit picturesque country churches steeped in history, grand mansions, thatched country cottages, historic sites, grand mansions, Roman villas, ancient burial mounds and much, much more. Along the way, you'll find pleasant walks, trails and towpaths, woodland footpaths and quiet country lanes to walk and explore.

Each route allows you to explore the countryside, visit attractions and, of course, stop for a cool beer and a spot of lunch or dinner.

Wootton Wawen

Wootton Wawen (pronounced Wowen) is a small village on the A3400, about 2 miles south of Henley-in-Arden and about 6.5 miles north of Stratford-upon-Avon. It's a neat little community that have to drive through on your way to Henley in Arden, so you might as well stop off along the way out from Stratford, or on your way on to Alcester, if that's the route you decide to take.

St. Peter's Church - Photo Courtesy of Creative Commons

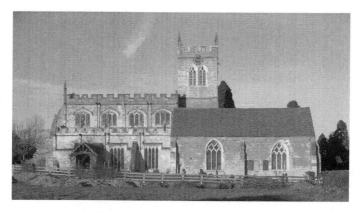

St. Peter's Church - Photo Courtesy of Creative Commons

There are several notable buildings in Wootton Wawen, the most important of which is parish church of Saint Peter, an Anglo-Saxon structure and the oldest church in Warwickshire - another is the Bull's Head Inn.

The church of Saint Peter features a chancel with a south chapel, nave, South aisle and the North tower, which is "embattled and pinnacled." There are also North and South porches, both extremely interesting for their stonework.

The base of the tower and the first two stages are Saxon with four doorways, the top of the tower is 15th century as are the clerestory, the nave battlements, the north doorway and porch, the middle arch of the arcade, the west window with busts of a king and queen and the east window with a leaf frieze. The tower is the earliest part of the church, preserved in the middle despite restricting views of the chancel from the nave, is the current site of the altar. The font is an octagonal bowl resting on eight sculptured heads; the old oak pulpit and choir screen is 15th century.

Chained Library St. Peter's Church - Photo Courtesy of Creative
Commons &

-

The church has a small chained library of 17th-century
theological works and some notable monumental brasses,
in particular the tomb of John Harewell and his wife Anna
that dates to 1505.

You should also take a moment to visit the aqueduct
on the Stratford Canal. It's quite impressive.

The Aqueduct on the Stratford Canal in Wootton Wawen - Photo
Courtesy of Creative Commons

Best Pubs:

Well, the Bull's Head Inn is located at the south end of
the street, a supposed 16th century L-shaped, timber-
framed structure with open fireplaces - one has a lintel
inscribed M 1697 TH - and open-timbered ceilings. There
is, however, a stone carved the date of the building as 1317.

The Bull's Head Pub in Wootton Wawen - Photo Courtesy of Creative Commons & Roy Hughes

Alcester

The market town of Alcester dates back to Roman times and is one of the most investigated small roman towns in the country. Follow Alcester's Heritage Trail and discover historic buildings, a selection of exciting pubs and tearooms, plus a wide choice of traditional, independent shops. Don't miss Roman Alcester, a museum which traces the town's links to the Romans and their continuing influence.

Alcester High Street on Market Day - Photo Courtesy of Creative Commons

In Roman times Alcester was a walled town and fort. It was an important town for the Romans because it was located at the confluence of several major roads: Ryknild Street Roman road, the ancient Saltway from Droitwich, the Roman road from Stratford upon Avon, and the Fosse Way.

There has been a settlement on the site where Alcester stands for more than 2,000 years, certainly before the Romans came to Britain. After the Norman Conquest in 1066, Ralph le Boteler, in the middle of the 12th century, founded a Benedictine monastery on the site. The town itself is a result of the monastery and was probably founded around 1272.

Today, Alcester is a thriving little town with a population of about 9,000 and lots to offer its many visitors. There are a number of well-preserved Tudor buildings and houses, most notably those near the parish church, in Butter Street and in Malt Mill Lane.

Malt Hill Lane - Photo Courtesy of Arian Perkins

The clock on St Nicholas' church is in an unusual position set on the edge of the south-west corner of the 14th century tower, making it visible from the main High Street. The church also houses the tomb of Fulke Greville, grandfather of Fulke Greville, 1st Baron Brooke. I suggest you take a quick peek inside the church; it's very interesting

Photo Courtesy of Stephen McKay

Sightseeing around Alcester

Ragley Hall

Near Alcester, be sure to visit Ragley and Coughton Court. Ragley is the family home of the Marquess and Marchioness of Hertford. See its fine collection of 18th century furniture and paintings and superb parkland containing the Jerwood Sculpture Park. The walk around the gardens is also a nice way to spend a quiet afternoon.

Ragley Hall - Photo Courtesy of David Fiddes

Opening Times:

Ragley Hall, Park & Gardens are closed during the winter months.

The Park and Gardens are open every Saturday and Sunday from March 22nd through October 25th 2014.

Ragley Hall is open for guided tours every Sunday from March 23rd until 25th October 2014.

Important Note: Ragley Hall is closed on Saturdays. Be sure to call ahead to check the current opening times at 01789 762 090 or you can check online at: http://www.ragley.co.uk/opening-times/

Admission:

Adult to park and gardens £8.50; guided tour of the Hall £2

Child aged 5 - 16 years   to park and gardens £5.50; guided tour of the Hall £1

Children under 5 years   Free

Ragley Hall is located just 2 miles South West of Alcester, just off the A435/A46, and 8 miles from Stratford-upon-Avon, also via the A46.

Coughton Court

The historic Coughton Court, and its extensive gardens, are well worth a visit. The imposing Tudor house is steeped in the Throckmorton family history and the glorious gardens include a rose labyrinth, lake and riverside walk. Its main claim to fame is the notorious Throckmorton Plot of 1583 to murder Queen Elizabeth I, and then its involvement in the Gunpowder Plot of 1605. The Throckmortons were only indirectly implicated in the plot, when the house became a refuge for some of the after its discovery.

Coughton Court Photo Courtesy of Creative Commons

Admission:

Whole Property

Adult: £9.60

Child: £4.80

Family: £24.00

Garden only

Adult: £6.30

Child: £3.10

Family: £15.80

Opening Times:

Cought Court is open most days, but there are some restricted days. Be sure to check online before you go at https://www.nationaltrust.org.uk/coughton-court/

How to Get There:

Coughton Court is about 2 ½ miles north of Alcester on the A435. You can see it from the road; you can't miss it.

Best Pubs in Alcester

The Bear

The Bear Hotel is a traditional pub located on High Street in Alcester, which makes it very convenient. I regularly pop into The Bear for lunch when I am in Alcester. The beer is always good, the atmosphere is typical of the English pub and is inviting.

The food is reasonably priced, home cooked, in-house (always a plus - many rely heavily on the freezer and micro-waver oven) and it's always piping hot. The staff I have always found to be very friendly and polite (another big plus).

Arrow Mill

I have mentioned this pub earlier in the section on Stratford, but there's no harm in mentioning it again here; it is, after located in Alcester. The beer is good, the food is even better. If you can, try eat dinner at Arrow Mill, you won't be disappointed: The setting is spectacular, the food is beyond compare, and the atmosphere is friendly and inviting. You will need to make a reservation: Phone 01789 762419

How to Get There

Alcester is located at the junction of the River Alne and River Arrow, approximately 8 miles west of Stratford-upon-Avon and about 11 miles from Wooton Wawen. From Stratford, take the A46 Alcester Road and drive on into Alcester. From Wootton Wawen, take the A3400 to its junction with A46 Alcester Road, turn right onto the A46 and drive on into Alcester.

The mediaeval market town of Henley in Arden originated as a clearing in the Forest of Arden and has a rich variety of architecture - red brick, black and white half-timber and plaster sit side by side and blend to give the town its unique character. The little town is set in a valley of the River Alne, which separates Henley from the adjacent settlement of Beaudesert. Did Shakespeare walk the streets of Henley? Certainly not the streets we know today, but I have no doubt that he knew the Henley of his day quite well.

Photo Courtesy of Creative Commons & David Stowell

No one knows for sure exactly when the small market town was established, but it is generally agreed that its founding dates to sometime during the 12th century. Henley was originally a hamlet of Wootton Wawen, on the original route out of the Forest of Arden.

John the Baptist Church - Photo Courtesy of Creative Commons & David Stowell

There are several historical buildings and structures, worth taking a look at in Henley, including the parish churches of St. Nicholas and St. John the Baptist, the 15th century Guildhall, the medieval market cross, the 16th century White Swan, and several half-timbered buildings and residences along High Street, the main street of the town, including the Elderly Building, which is one of the most unique frontages I have ever seen. And there are a couple of nice pubs, but more about those in the next section.

The Elderly Building - Photo Courtesy of Creative Commons & Chris Allen

The Nag's Head - Photo Courtesy of Creative Commons & David Stowell

Best Pubs

If I had to choose a favorite pub in Henley, just for a pint of beer, it would be the Nag's Head on High Street (see photo above). It's a nice pub, friendly and the beer is good, and you can't say fairer than that.

The Bluebell

And then there's the Bluebell on High Street: "The Bluebell is your everyday treat!" That's what they say, and who could argue?

The Bluebell Pub - Photo Courtesy of Creative Commons & Kenneth Allen

The Bluebell is a "free house," which means it's not owned by a brewery and can thus sell any brand of beer it likes, and it offers some really good beers: "Craft beers, local cask ales from Purity, Hook Norton, Wye Valley & The Shed," and more.

The Bluebell is open for lunch from noon or dinner from 6pm; choose from traditional English pies, crispy fish & chips, really good sandwiches, or from the "good value menu du jour."

Afternoon Tea (always a delight) is served between 3.30pm – 5pm.

If you happen to be in Stratford over a weekend, you should try to make it over to the Bluebell for Sunday lunch. These folks know how to cook a roast: free-range pork & crackling or roast Sirloin of Aubrey Allen's 32 day aged Scottish beef with Yorkshire Pudding and baked cauliflower cheese… yummy.

How to Get There

Henley-in-Arden (Henley to those who live round about) is approximately 2 miles from Wooton Wawen, 9 miles west of Warwick and 9 miles north of Stratford upon Avon. The town is at a crossroads between the A3400 and the A4189 roads

West from Stratford

Most of the towns and villages in the west Warwickshire can be visited piecemeal from Stratford. There are several options, however, that I recommend you dedicate a full day to. These include the historic market town of Evesham and its surrounds, and the Eastern Cotswolds. To spend time in Stratford and not do these day trips would, in my opinion, wonderful opportunities missed. They are easy to do by car. Everything is quite close together, and the round trip from Stratford is not more than 45 miles for any of the trips. You can do most of them in a half a day, if you want to, but that, I think, would not do them justice. Take the time out and enjoy yourself.

Two Day Trips to the Cotswolds

I've split the Cotswolds into two distinct and separate days out from Stratford, or from London. You can choose the option that you think will suite you best, and then plan your day out accordingly, or you could dedicate a couple of days to the Cotswolds and see it all.

The Cotswolds Option 1

This tour takes in the Rollright Stones (a much smaller version of Stonehenge), Chipping Campden and Broadway.

The Rollright Stones

I have placed this attraction first in this section because, if you're making the trip by car, you'll probably pass by it on the way to Chipping Campden.

The Rollrights are an attraction you'll not find in many guide books. I used to visit the Rollrights when I was a child and, when they were old enough, I took my kids too. It's well worth a visit, and it's fun. Not only that, if you're driving in from London, to Chipping Campden or

Broadway, you have to pass by the site, so it just makes sense to stop off along the way.

The King's Men - Copyright © Blair Howard

The Rollright Stones are part of a Neolithic site whose origins lost in the mists of time. The old legends claim that the stones once were an ancient king and his knights turned to stone by a witch. The site has three main elements: the Kings Men stone circle, the King Stone, and the Whispering Knights.

The Rollright Stones are, in fact, a henge. Though not as spectacular as the more famous Stonehenge, but a henge is what it is. The main circle, the King's Men, measures about 100 feet in diameter and is set on top of a small ridge just off the main road.

Now, you can believe it or not, but there is definitely a certain air of ancient mystery about this site. I remember when I used to visit that it was a very quiet spot, lacking even the sounds of the countryside – birds singing, the chirping and buzzing of insects, and so on. Well... maybe, maybe not; you'll have to judge for yourself.

One local legend has it that it's impossible to accurately count the number of stones in the circle. Maybe that's because of the numerous small stones, many of them partially hidden by the long grass and thus easily missed. Try it, it's fun, and I bet you come up with a half dozen different counts.

The King Stone – Courtesy of Creative Commons

Just across the road from the Kings Men is the King
Stone, a solitary monolith much bigger than those in the
main circle. A few hundred yards further on along the path,
you'll find another small group of stones, the Whispering
Knights. This site once was "a turf-clad burial chamber."

The Whispering Knights – Courtesy of Brian Robert
Marshall & Creative Commons

I really do recommend you take a few moments to stop
by and visit. It's interesting, fun and a great photo op.

The Rollright Stones are located right on the
Oxfordshire/ Warwickshire border just off the A44 close to
Long Compton. Traveling from London to Chipping
Campden you'll be on the A44; watch for the signs.
There's a small admission charge £1 (50p for children)
which goes towards maintenance.

Chipping Campden

Chipping Campden, is the epitome of the small, Cotswold market town. Set within the Cotswold district of Gloucestershire, Chipping Campden can trace its roots all the way back to the 7th century and there's no doubt that the area was inhabited even before that during Neolithic times. In the 11th century, after the Norman conquest of England, it was recorded in King William's Domesday Book that the village had a population of 300.

In 1185, King Henry II granted a market charter to the then Lord of the manor, Hugh de Gondeville, and thus Campden became Chipping Campden, chipping being the old English word for market.

The original layout of Chipping Campden's elegant terraced High Street was designed by de Gondeville, but most of the architecture you see today dates from the 14th century to the 17th century.

In 1380, William Grevel, a local sheep merchant, and one of the richest men in England, built for himself a house on the High Street. That house, Grevel House, still stands today. The Woolstapler's Hall was built a little later by Robert Calf, another big wheel in the local wool industry.

You'll absolutely love this quaint little town. I spent many an evening frequenting one pub or the other, and many's the Saturday afternoon I rummaged through the books at the Campden Bookstore.

What to See

To walk the High Street is a singular delight. An avenue of honey-colored limestone buildings, built from the mellow locally quarried oolitic limestone known as Cotswold stone, it boasts a wealth of fine vernacular architecture. At its center stands the Market Hall with its splendid arches, built in 1627.

The Market Hall – Courtesy Creative Commons

Chipping Campden was a rich wool trading center during the Middle Ages, and enjoyed the patronage of many a wealthy wool merchant.

Today, Chipping Campden is a popular Cotswold tourist destination, and the starting point for the Cotswold Trail, a walking trail that stretches for 102 miles all the way to City of Bath. At times, especially on weekends, it can be very busy; the pubs, tea rooms, restaurants and shops especially so, but Chipping Campden is an attraction not to be missed.

Be sure to take in the grand, early perpendicular wool church of St James with its medieval altar frontals that date to the 14th century, its cope – 13th century - and its extravagant 17th century monuments to local wealthy silk merchant Sir Baptist Hicks and his family

Above you see the Church of St. James and the ruins of Campden House which was destroyed by fire during the English Civil War possibly to prevent it falling into the hands of the Parliamentarians. All that remains of this once magnificent estate are two gatehouses, two Jacobean banqueting houses, restored by the Landmark Trust, and Lady Juliana's gateway. Photo Credit: – Colin Craig .

Banqueting House & St. James' Church – Courtesy W. Lloyd MacKenzie

St. James' Church – Courtesy Stephen McKay

Take a quick peek at the Almshouses and Woolstaplers Hall. The gates to Campden House and the one-time wagon wheel wash, The Court Barn near the church is now a museum celebrating the rich Arts and Crafts tradition of the area.

The Alms Houses - Courtesy David Stowel

The Gates to Campden House; the old wagon wheel
wash is the depressed area at the right of the photo -
Courtesy David Stowel

The Campden Bookshop in Dragon House on the High Street has been a fascinating attraction for as long as I can remember. The shop offers a wide selection of guide books, books on the local Arts & Crafts Movement, art, and so on; it's also a fun place to just browse.

Best Pubs:

No visit to Chipping Campden would be complete without a cool pint of beer and pub lunch. That being so, you might like to sample the fare at the delightful little Eight Bells pub on Church Street or the Kings Arms on High Street.

The Eight Bells – Courtesy Stephen McKay

There are two famous and historic gardens nearby: at Hidcote Manor Garden, owned and managed by the National Trust, and at Kiftsgate, in private ownership but open to the public. Two miles to the west, in the grounds of Weston Park near Saintbury, are the earthwork remains of a motte and bailey castle.

The Ebrington Arms:

An old haunt of mine, the Ebrington Arms is a country pub specializing in fine dining. Known locally for the quality of its beer (very important) and for its excellent cuisine, old-world atmosphere and friendly owners – Claire and Jim Alexander – the Ebrington Arms is top of my list of places to eat. Be sure to make a reservation. 01386-593223.

The Eight Bells:

The Eight Bells, on Church Street, pictured above, is a 14th century traditional Cotswold Inn featuring a nice menu of good food offered daily for lunch and dinner. Reservations: 01386-840371

Huxley's Café and Wine Bar:

A "period Café and wine bar" on Chipping Campden's High Street is just the place for a nice lunch or an afternoon tea with fancy cakes and a cup of tea or coffee. 01386-849077

Broadway

From Chipping Campden, take the B4081 to its junction with the A-44 and drive on to the tiny Cotswold village of Broadway.

In the photo above you see Broadway's main street looking from north to south: The Swan Inn is at the left of picture as you look at it; the village green is behind the lamppost at right and you can just see the Broadway Hotel at the extreme right. This photo was taken in the mid 1960s, but it could have been taken yesterday; little has changed. Photo courtesy of Creative Commons.

Broadway claims to be the most beautiful village in England and, looking at the image on the next page, who could argue? Broadway is, perhaps, the quintessential Cotswold village.

The natural stone cottages, and elegant homes, house many of England's rich and famous. The cottages were built mostly in the early 17th century and are maintained today just as they were 300 years ago.

The photo above is a view of Broadway's main street -
Courtesy of Trevor Rickard .

The Broad Way, or main street, features many antique
shops, art galleries, craft shops, pubs and tea rooms... and
it's sad to say that Broadway, over the past 50 years or so,
may have become the quintessential Cotswold tourist trap.
Prices for all things, large and small, are higher in
Broadway than almost anywhere else in the region. Be that
as it may, Broadway is a delight and a must visit, just be
careful and make sure you're getting value for money.

No visit to Broadway would be complete without a
visit to the Tower. The top of the Tower is the highest point
in the Cotswolds, and the view from the top is the best of
more than 100 such views. Even from the foot of the
Tower, the view over the Vale of Evesham is stunning;
from the top, it's unbelievable.

What to See:

Broadway Tower

Copyright © Blair Howard

The Tower was designed by James Wyatt in 1798 for the sixth Earl of Coventry, who probably had more money than sense. The Tower is built in the Norman style with three turrets and is surrounded by parkland. You can drive up the hill from Broadway, or you can hike it via a short section of the Cotswold Way: through the fields and kissing gates and over the wooden styles to the top, and then down again; it's a round-trip walk of about 5 ½ miles; allow at least three hours.

The Shops on the Broadway

It's claimed that Broadway "has one of the longest village High Streets in the UK." I don't know if that's true, but it is quite a hike from the north end at the Swan Inn to the south end at the foot of Fish Hill. The lower high street is where you'll find all the shops, restaurants and tea shops;

116

the upper high street offers photo ops of this quintessential Cotswold village: tiny, honey-colored cottages, some with thatched roofs, and grand old houses, all vying with one another to grow the best flower gardens, and grow them they do.

Church of St Eadburgha

The original parish church of Broadway, the Church of St Eadburgha, has been a Christian place of worship since the 12th century. The current church was built around 1400 but there are elements that remain of the original 12th century building. The dedication of a Christian church to Eadburgha is not common. Eadburgha was the grand-daughter of Alfred the Great. As a child Eadburgha was asked to choose between receiving jewels or her own Bible, she chose the Bible. The church is listed as an English Heritage Grade I English Heritage Building.

Church of St. Eadburgha – Courtesy of Creative Commons

Where to Eat

Russell's

Following on from the last entry, Russell's has, since it open a few years ago, gained a reputation as one of the finest restaurants in the area, so say my relatives and friends that visit on a regular basis. Add Russell's Fish and Chip Shop just next at Number 20a, and you have the best of both worlds.

Fish & Chips is, of course, the English staple, and Russell's serve only the finest fish. You can eat in or take away, and the shop is open for Lunch and Dinner from 12noon-2.30pm and 5.00-8.30pm, Tuesday through Saturday – closed Sunday and Monday.

The **Swan Inn** at the north end of High Street, opposite the Village Green, offers good food at reasonable prices, as does the **Broadway Hotel** at the west side of the green.

If afternoon tea is what you're craving, well… you might like to try **Tisanes Tea Rooms** at Cotswold House on the Green where, so I'm told, Tracey and Steve will provide "a nice pot of tea or coffee with cakes, sandwiches and soft drinks.

Best Pubs

Nothing is more refreshing on warm summer day that a cool pint of local beer; better yet, nothing is more refreshing than an ice-cold pint of shandy – beer and lemonade mixed together in equal parts. Broadway has several nice pubs, including the **Broadway Hotel**, the **Swan Inn** and my favorite haunt, the **Horse and Hound** on upper High Street. Another of my old haunts is the **Crown and Trumpet** on Church Street, just off the Village Green on the left. It's been a while since I was last in there, but I have a feeling it's changed very little: great pint of beer, and quiet.

This trip will take you a little father to the west visiting Burford and Bourton on the Water.

Burford

Burford is another of those historic, little market towns for which the Cotswolds are so famous. And small it is, with a population of just over 1,000, it's a sleepy town that owes it wealth and fame to the wool trade. Located just 20 miles west of Oxford on the A40, and less that 10 miles from Stow on the Wold, Bourton on the Water and Northleach, Burford is your southern gateway into the Cotswolds.

It doesn't get much nicer than this. The scene in the photo above is of Burford High Street on a sunny afternoon in winter – Courtesy of John Shortland .

No one is quite sure when the area was first settled, but it seems likely that people have inhabited what is now Burford since Neolithic times. The Domesday Book, 1086, William the Conqueror's tally of his new possessions in England records a small village of approximately 200. The little community was granted a charter to hold markets either in the late 11th or early 12th Centuries, exactly when, no one seems to know.

Today, Burford is a popular stop along the way into the Cotswolds. A busy, though unspoiled little community, its businesses have a "long tradition of good service and the supply of excellent luxury and essential goods to both residents and visitors."

Sheep Street, Burford – Courtesy of Martin Bodman & Creative Commons

Burford's High Street, not so very different from its Costwold peers, is lined with the old houses and cottages so typical of the area – all built from the same honey-colored stone. Burford is timeless; a microcosm of narrow side streets and alleyways separating the 17th and 18th Century buildings. Tiny shops, tea rooms, art galleries and antiques shops offer a wealth of treasures and opportunities to enjoy that oh-so-typical English afternoon tea and cakes.

121

You'll also want to visit the splendid parish church, more cathedral than church, a product of the wealth that came to Burford during the era of the Cotswold wool trade

One of Burford's Alleyways – Courtesy Andy F & Creative Commons

St John the Baptist Church, in Burford,

Wealth from wool gave the parish church of Saint John the Baptist its current grandeur. The building was completed in the late 1400s and its windows filled with stained glass, of which only fragments remain. The widows you see today are restorations carried out during the early part of the 20th Century.

Church of John the Baptist, Burford – Courtesy of
Colin Smith & Creative Commons

The Whall Window in the Church of John the Baptist –
Courtesy of David Stowell & Creative Commons

Finally, you'll want to stroll the banks of the tiny River
Windrush that meanders through the town; the same River
Windrush you'll visit at Bourton on the Water.

The River Windrush at Burford – Courtesy of David
Stowell & Creative Commons

Yes, Burford is, indeed, a beautiful little town. A fact
that's not in dispute as Burford has been designated an
Area of Outstanding Natural Beauty and is protected by the
Cotswolds Conservation Board.

Burford is perfectly placed as base to explore the other
famous towns and villages of the surrounding area
including Oxford and Cheltenham and other attractions too.

Best Pubs:

The Mermaid Inn, Burford – Courtesy of Colin Smith
& Creative Commons

The Lamb Inn, Burford – Courtesy of Peter Watkins &
Creative Commons

Bourton-on-the-Water, one of the Cotswolds' most visited destinations, is a personal favorite of mine. I, literally, could not even hazard a guess as to how many times I've visited this quaint, old-world and visually appealing little town. My mother used to take me to Bourton when I was a small child, and I in turn would take my own children; I still visit when Bourton whenever I can.

The River Windrush - Courtesy of Keith Fairhurst

Bourton-on-the-Water is just 12 miles from Burford: take the A424 to its junction with the A429 (the Fosse Way) turn left and drive on into Bourton.

Bourton-on-the-Water is named for the tiny river upon which it sits. The river Windrush is a delightful little waterway, a tinkling brook or creek that runs directly through the center of town. Along the way, a series of picturesque, low stone bridges provide access to the shops

127

and cafes on one side of the river or the other. The riverbank is lined with trees, neatly-trimmed lawns and honey-colored Cotswold stone banks.

The River Windrush at Bourton-on-the-Water –
Courtesy of Saffron Blaze

All of the buildings that line the streets are built from the same honey-colored stone, most of them dating back to the 17th Century. Many of the old homes remain while others have been converted into small, intimate shops and restaurants. Bourton, today, is an important center for tourism and, sadly, perhaps a little more commercial than many of the villagers would like. Even so, the villagers do their best to make Bourton a fun place to visit

Cotswold Stone Cottages in Bourton-on-the-Water - Courtesy of David Barnes .

Bourton-on-the-Water Attractions

The main attraction, at least for me, is the river Windrush. To sit and watch the water tinkling by on warm summer afternoon is a treat; to walk the riverbanks at sunset, or even sunrise, is a rare treat, and to enjoy the waterside view along with a pint of local beer at the Old Manse pub is a treat I could not begin to describe. Try it. I think you'll agree.

Birdland

Birdland Park and Gardens, established by Len Hill, is home of some 600 species of birds, including a remarkable collection of penguins. There's also and a large pond full of fish – yes, you can feed them – the staff also present Birds of Prey and penguin feeding. It's a fun place to visit; many of the birds are allowed to fly loose among the trees.

King Penguins at Birdland Courtesy of Christine
Matthews

The Model Village

The Model Village, one of the most popular of
Bourton's attractions, is located behind the Old New Inn.
The model, built by local craftsmen in the 1930s, and
opened in 1937, is an exact replica of Bourton-on-the-
Water. It's built of natural Cotswold stone to one-ninth
scale. For a small fee, you can become Gulliver for a day
and wander the streets of this miniature village at will.

The Model Village - Courtesy of Adrian Pingstone

Other attractions include a perfume factory and model railway exhibition.

Bourton is also the confluence of several long-distance walks, including the Cotswold Way, and the Heart of England Way, a 100-mile hike that actually finishes in the village.

Best Pub:

The Mousetrap Inn

With a name like that, how could it not be a great pub? Well, it is, and I can recommend it. They serve good old English "pub grub." and local English ales. Pub Grub? In this case it means they still serve the traditional Ploughman's lunch in the summer time and good hot stews and puddings in the winter. Yes, you can get a steak if you want - vegetarians are also catered for - and breakfast is available each morning; dinner is served Tuesday through Saturday.

Visit the Cotswolds by Guided Tour

Premier Tours out of London offer several guided tours to the Cotswolds. Go to premiertours.co.uk

Evesham is a small market town in Worcestershire, just on the northern edge of the Cotswolds. The town was founded sometime during the end of the 7th Century, the late 600s. Over the past 100 years, or so, there's been quite a bit of controversy about how the town came by its name. It's not worth going into in depth here, but to most local folk Evesham is a derivative of the combination of two Old English words Eof and Homme (or Ham): Eof being the name of a swineherd in the service of Egwin, third bishop of Worcester and Homme meaning home, thus you would have the name Eof's Home or *Eveshomme* as recorded in 709. And as *Evesham* in 1086.

The legend tells us that Eof, while tending his pigs, had a vision of the Virgin Mary; Bishop Egwin is said to have built the great Benedictine Abbey at Evesham on that spot starting around the year 701. The Abbey was enlarged after the Norman Conquest and became one of the largest in England, but it fell victim to King Henry VIII's Dissolution of the abbeys and was demolished in 1540; only the great Bell Tower and parts of the abbey wall, including Cloisters Gateway remain; all are located in the Abbey Park and they alone are worth the visit.

Things to See in Evesham:

Abbot Clement Litchfield's Bell Tower

The Bell Tower dominates the Evesham skyline. It's an iconic structure built around 1530 to hold the bells of Evesham Abbey. The tower was commissioned by Abbot Clement Lichfield, the last abbot of Evesham. The Bell Tower is located close to where the north transept of the great Abbey Church once stood. The Church and almost all

133

the monastic buildings were demolished in 1540 as part of the Dissolution by King Henry VIII. By all accounts, the Kings men entered the abbey during Evensong of January 30th. The monks were ejected and demolition began quickly after.

The Bell Tower by Moonlight – Copyright © Blair Howard

The Bell Tower survived the Dissolution; why is a matter of some conjecture: Some think it may have been because the people of Evesham had contributed to the cost of its construction; others will tell you it was a gift to the town from the King; some say that it was purchased from the King by the town for the sum of £100; the real reason is lost in the mists of time.

The Bell Tower in Daylight – Courtesy of Creative Commons

The Churchyard of All Saints and St. Lawrence

The Bell Tower today stands between the Abbey Churchyard and the Abbey Gardens, or Park, with an archway through the tower itself. The churchyard is unique in that it's the only one that I know of that contains two churches.

The Two Churches of St. Lawrence (left) and All Saints – Copyright © Blair Howard

The two churches, St Lawrence and All Saints were built by the Benedictine monks of Evesham Abbey in the 12th century to serve the people of Evesham. Abbot Clement Lichfield is buried in the Church of All Saints. Today, the two fine buildings, along with the adjacent Abbot Reginald's Gateway, present a wealth of photo opportunities.

Abbot Reginald's Gateway:

Abbot Reginald's Gateway is the walkway from the town's market square into the churchyard of All Saints and St. Lawrence and the Bell Tower and Abbey Park beyond. Part of the gateway – the lower walls, date to early Norman times; the upper buildings, probably 16th century, once were the vicarage.

Abbot Reginald's Gateway – Copyright © Blair Howard

137

Today, the gateway houses a tea room that bears the same name (lunch, afternoon tea and cakes) and a small antique shop. The Gateway, from both sides, presents a nice photo op, especially in winter when the snow is on the ground and the buildings.

The Almonry:

Located just outside the churchyard of All Saints and St. Lawrence churches, this 14th Century building was once home to the Almoner of the great Benedictine Abbey. The almoner of the abbey was the monk charged with looking after the poor and destitute of the town. Following the Dissolution of the Abbey, the Almonry became the personal home of the abbot; whatever else was left of the Abbey buildings were sold to Sir Philip Hoby.

The Almonry and Stocks – Copyright © Blair Howard

The Almonry, over the past 475 years, has been many things to many people: a public house, tea rooms, even a private home. Finally, in 1929, the Almonry was purchased by Evesham Borough Council and, in 1957, it was opened to the public as a museum owned and funded by the

Evesham town council and operated by the Vale of Evesham Historical Society.

Today the Almonry houses a wealth of information and artefacts, documenting such important happenings as the history of the great Abbey and the defeat of Baron Simon de Montfort at the Battle of Evesham in 1265. You can also view the abbot's great chair, a 14th century psalter (bible), and the famous Matthew Bible dated to 1537. The museum also houses relics from the Neolithic period to the present day, including Anglo-Saxon burial treasure, and artifacts from the Civil War.

The Abbey Park, Gardens and Cloisters Arch:

The park and gardens are best accessed through Abbot Reginald's Gateway in the Market Place.

The Abbey Gardens-Courtesy Bill Johnson

You can view the two churches, walk through the arch under the Bell Tower, and on down to the riverbank. It's a nice, short walk and interesting too.

The Cloisters Arch – Copyright © Blair Howard

The Cloisters Arch is just to the right of the Bell Tower as you enter into the park from the churchyard, no more than 20 yards, or so. The arch dates to the 12th century and is interesting for its many carvings.

Offenham

Ok, that's it for this section of the trip. From Evesham, we'll drive about three miles to Offenham.

In Evesham, take Port Street south to Elm Road and bear left, then turn left on Offenham Road and drive on a couple of miles into Offenham.

By now, it's probably time for lunch and there are two pubs where we can do just that: The Bridge Inn and the Fish and Anchor. Both pubs are on the riverbank and both are nice places to take a short break.

My personal favorite is the Bridge Inn. I have spent countless weekend hours there: lunchtimes on Saturdays and Sundays, and Friday and Saturday evenings; it's just a very pleasant spot to sit back for a few minutes and relax over a sandwich and cool pint of beer. From Main Street, take Boat Lane to the Bridge Inn.

The Bridge Inn at Offenham – Courtesy of David Luther Thomas

The Fish and Anchor does not have river access for boats, but it's also a nice place to eat lunch. You'll find it just out of Offenham on the B4510.

The view of the river is pleasant, and the food is good too.

Middle Little Tithe Barn

From Offenham, it's just a short drive of another three miles to Middle Littleton. Take the B4510 from Offenham, then turn left on Cleeve Road about 4/10 mile and turn left onto school lane and drive another 3/10 mile to the Tithe Barn and the Church.

The Tithe Barn is the main reason for this visit. It's one of the largest and certainly one of the finest 13th-century tithe barns in the country. It was built for the monks of Evesham Abbey, mostly of the local Cotswold stone. The barn measures some 130 feet in length and approximately 42 feet wide. This type of Tithe barn was used during the Middle Ages for storing the tithes received from the church's tenant farmers - a tenth of the farm's produce. In this case, Evesham Abbey.

The Great Tithe Barn at Middle Littleton – Courtesy of Phillip Halling

The National Record says that the Barn was built in 1376 by Abbot John Ombersley of Evesham, but the National Trust, the organization that looks after the building, gives the date as much earlier in the 13th century, probably as result of radiocarbon testing that dates the construction at around 1250.

The interior woodwork is amazing, especially the hammer-beam truss-work supporting the roof. Middle Littleton's Tithe barn truly is a magnificent building, and a monument to the medieval craftsmen and engineers that built it. The barn is open seven days a week.

The Interior of the Tithe barn Showing Construction
Details-Photo Courtesy of Creative Commons

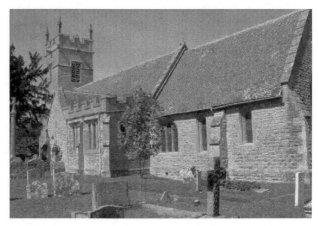

The Church of St. Nicholas at Middle Littleton –
Courtesy of Phillip Halling

St Nicholas' Church, situated between North and
Middle Littleton parishes, is just a few yards walk from the
Great Tithe barn, and it's worth a quick look while you're
there.

Bretforton

The Fleece Inn at Bretforton is the next stop on our
trip. Take the B4085 west to Blackminster and turn left
onto Station Road and drive on into Bretforton, about 4
miles.

The Fleece Inn at Bretforton – Courtesy of Roger Davis

Many's the pleasant evening I have spent supping a pint, or two, in the old Fleece Inn. This magnificent public house is more than 600 years old, and has been a pub since 1848. The inn was badly damaged by a fire in 2004, but has since been restored to its former glory and is now owned by the National Trust, which gives you some idea of how important the Fleece is considered to be.

Wickhamford

The final stop on the tour is Wickhamford. Take the B4035 Badsey-Bretforton road north out of Bretforton and turn right onto Badsey High Street, turn left onto School Lane, then right onto Golden Lane, and then left on Manor Road.

The Manor House – Copyright © Blair Howard

The object of this trip is Wickhamford's tiny church, and its contents.

St John the Baptist Church, Wickhamford is located at the north of the village, next to the manor house.

Church of John the Baptist – Copyright © Blair Howard

Typical of most English country churches, the door of St. John the Baptist is usually open. You can simply walk inside and browse around undisturbed. Built early in the 12th century, it's an odd little Norman church with a tower instead of a steeple. When full, which it rarely is, it will seat maybe 60 people. There's no altar as such, just a fine antique table covered with a red velvet cloth. The vestments consist of a couple of candle sticks and a simple silver cross. The sanctuary is dominated by a magnificent, canopied monument to the Sandys family.

Sir Edwyn Sandys, a great English parliamentarian, was Treasurer of the Virginia Company during the reign of King James I, and it was through his influence that the first representative assembly in America met at Jamestown in 1619.

The Sandys Monument inside Wickhamford Church –
Copyright © Blair Howard

Other than the Sandys monument, there seems to be little else within the church to interest the visitor. But then, however, you might spot the small table just inside the main lobby. On it you will find a stack of small, informational booklets. These contain a brief history of the church. The booklet has only a half-dozen pages, and it's free. If you like, you can drop a small donation in the box provided. On the last page of that little book, in the second-to-last paragraph, you will learn that American visitors might be interested in the "floor-slab" monument located within the altar rails.

You would surely be forgiven for not spotting the slab sooner, for it's concealed beneath a large red rug that covers the floor beneath the altar table.

Step through the tiny gate in the altar rail - don't worry, no one will mind if you're careful - and pull back the rug, you will find a large stone slab set into the floor. It's perhaps six feet long by three feet wide.

The inscription on the slab is in Latin. It tells of the piety and virtue, and the generosity of the lady whose body lies beneath the slab, Penelope Washington. Penelope was the daughter of Colonel Henry Washington, a royalist hero of the English civil war. She also was a cousin the first American president, George Washington. Worth a visit? I think so, I hope you will too.

By the way, the village pub, The Sandys Arms, is famous for its "bar food," and the village itself is as pretty as they come, a fair ending to our day out.

From Wickhamford, it a drive of about three miles back to Broadway, say 10 miles to Chipping Campden.

Thank You:

I sincerely hope you enjoyed this book. Thank you so much for downloading it. If you have comments of questions, you can contact me by email. I will reply to all emails. And you can also visit my website for a complete list of my books. If you enjoyed the book, I would really appreciate it if you could take a few moments and share your thoughts by posting a review on Amazon.

Other Books by this Author:

Visitor's Guides:

Visitor's Guide to London

The Visitor's Guide to the English Cotswolds

The Visitor's Guide to Bermuda:

A Complete Guide to the Islands

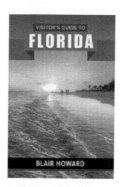

The Visitor's Guide to Florida:

A Complete Guide to the Sunshine State

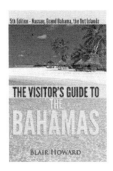

The Visitor's Guide to the Bahamas 5th Edition:

The Collection (All three books in one)

The Visitor's Guide to the Bahamas:

The Out Islands: The Abacos, The Exumas, Eleuthera, The Acklins and More

Civil War Books

Battlefields of the Civil War Vol 1:

Visitor's Guide

Great Battles of the American Civil War

Chickamauga

Touring Southern Civil War Battlefields: From
Vicksburg to Savannah

Photography Books:

152

How to Take Better Photographs:

Quick and Simple Tips for Improving Your
Photographs

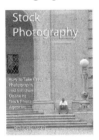

Stock Photography:

How to take Great Photographs and Sell them Online
to Stock Photo Agencies

The Photo Essay:

The How to Make Money with your Camera Guide for
Writers and Photographers:

Digital Photography - Understanding Composition

Made in the USA
San Bernardino, CA
13 March 2014